TRIBUTES

TO THE

SCARLET RIDERS

An anthology of Mountie poems

Collected by

Edgar A. Kuhn

Heritage
House

NANOOSE • VANCOUVER

National Library of Canada Cataloguing in Publication

Tributes to the scarlet riders: an anthology of Mountie
poems / collected by Edgar Kuhn.

ISBN 1-894384-70-9

1. Royal Canadian Mounted Police—Poetry. I. Kuhn, Edgar A., 1932–

PS8287.R69T75 2003   C811.008'03523632   C2003-905731-3

First edition 2003

Heritage House acknowledges the financial support for our publishing
program from the Government of Canada through the Book Publishing
Industry Development Program (BPIDP), Canada Council for the Arts, and
the British Columbia Arts Council.

Every effort was made to acquire permission to reprint the poems in this
book. We welcome any information that would allow us to correct any
errors or omissions in a subsequent edition.

Cover and book design by Nancy St.Gelais
Edited by Karla Decker

HERITAGE HOUSE PUBLISHING COMPANY LTD.
Unit #108 – 17665 66A Ave., Surrey, BC V3S 2A7

Printed in Canada

The Canada Council | Le Conseil des Arts
for the Arts | du Canada

Dedicated to
the brave members of
the Mounted Police, past and present,
so vital to forging our nation.

ACKNOWLEDGEMENTS

Just prior to the Royal Canadian Mounted Police centennial celebrations in 1973, Mrs. Isabelle Eaglesham of Weyburn, Saskatchewan, began collecting many of these old poems. She was president of the Saskatchewan History and Folklore Society, was herself a noted historian and author, and was very much inspired by her centennial project. I was in charge of the Weyburn RCMP detachment in 1973 when she approached me with her project; however, I was not able to assist her at that time. A selection of her poems was first printed in a book titled *Wake the Prairie Echoes* (Saskatchewan History and Folklore Society, 1973). A few years ago she presented her collection to me to do with as I may, and I have added to it a fair number of poems that I collected personally over the years. My deep gratitude to Mrs. Eaglesham and the Saskatchewan History and Folklore Society cannot be adequately expressed here.

Many of the poems' authors have passed away, could not be traced, or were simply unknown. Regimental numbers, where known, have been shown after the authors' names. I would be glad to receive information about any of the authors cited as "Anonymous."

The North West Mounted Police force (NWMP) was born May 20,1873, by order-in-council of the federal parliament in Ottawa. In 1905, the force became the Royal North West Mounted Police (RNWMP), and in 1920 it acquired its present name, the Royal Canadian Mounted Police (RCMP). These poems are a legacy of the NWMP, RNWMP and present RCMP eras. They cover a wide spectrum of the early history of Canada's "wild west" in stories of heroism, emotions, hardships, dedication, loyalty, respect and the human element. Intended to stir imagination, admiration, and excitement in the mind of the reader, I hope they will be appreciated and enjoyed.

I acknowledge with gratitude the poems that appeared in *Wake the Prairie Echoes, Scarlet and Gold,* and *RCMP Quarterly* many years ago. I also extend my thanks to the Kamloops RCMP Veterans' Association for its assistance. As well, I extend my heartfelt thanks to my daughter, Angela, who worked diligently on this project, and to many others who offered their assistance and encouragement.

Sergeant Edgar Arthur Kuhn (Rtd.)
Weyburn, Saskatchewan

FOREWORD

When modern-day members of the Force require inspiration and strength in times of crisis, they often invoke the sacrifices, accomplishments and spirit of those members who have gone before. The long and storied history of Canada's national police force is full of folklore, mythology, and good humour, but also, all too often, sadness and tragedy. Ed Kuhn's anthology of *Tributes to the Scarlet Riders* captures all of those elements.

It has always struck me as odd that some of the most famous episodes in the history of the Mounted Police have focused on human failings, but at the same time, they do reflect the humanity of those front-line police officers who did the very best they could to live up to the challenges of their offices and their times. *Tributes to the Scarlet Riders* is no exception in that the stories come alive with the hopes, dreams, aspirations and pride of being Canadians and members of the Force.

Tributes to the Scarlet Riders serves a serious purpose in that it reveals the perceptions of those inside the Force and those observing it at different times over history. But it is not a serious book. There is much fun to be had in reading many of the tales conveyed in the anthology. So, find a comfortable chair, sit back and enjoy Ed Kuhn's *Tributes to the Scarlet Riders*.

J.P.R. (Phil) Murray
Commissioner (Rtd.)
Ottawa, March, 2003

CONTENTS

The Arctic

Recruits, Training, and Horses

Life and Duty

Tall Tales and True Stories

Tributes to the Force and its Veterans

The Mounties' Early Years (1873–1905)

The Riders of the Plains

—W. S., NWMP

Probably the best-known poem about the Force, "The Riders of the Plains" appeared as early as 1878 in the Saskatchewan Herald *at Battleford and later in* RCMP Quarterly, *1963, and* Wake the Prairie Echoes. *The original version was added to several times over a period of years, and one contributor was believed to be Sub-Constable Thomas A. Boys, who took his discharge in 1878 and became a lawyer in Calgary, Alberta. The* Saskatchewan Herald *credited it only to "W.S. NWMP." The poem is a rousing, blood-stirring tribute to the bravery and dedication of the first Mounties.*

Oh! Wake the prairie echoes, the ever-welcome sound,
Ring out the "boots and saddle" till the stirring notes resound.
Our chargers toss their bridled heads and chafe against the reins,
Ring out, ring out the marching call, The Riders of the Plains.

O'er many a league of prairie wild, our trackless path must be,
And round it roam the fiercest tribes of Blackfoot and of Cree.
But danger from their treacherous hands a dauntless heart disdains;
'Tis the heart that bears the helmet of, The Riders of the Plains.

The prairie storms sweep o'er our way, but onward still we go,
To scale the weary mountain range, descend the valley low.
We face the broad Saskatchewan made fierce with heavy rains,
With all his might he cannot check, The Riders of the Plains.

We tread the dreaded cactus land, where lost to white man's ken,
We startle there the creatures wild with sight of armed men.
For whereso'er our leader bids, the bugle sounds its strains,
Forward in marching sections go, The Riders of the Plains.

The Fire King stalks the prairie, and fearful 'tis to see
The rushing wall of smoke and flame surrounds us rapidly.
'Tis there we shout defiance and mark his fiery chains,
For safe the cleared circle guards, The Riders of the Plains.

For us no cheerful hostelries, their welcome gates unfold;
No generous board, no downy couch, await the troops bold.
Beneath the starry canopy are we when daylight wanes;
There lie the hardy wanderers, The Riders of the Plains.

In want of rest, in want of food, our courage does not fail,
As day and night we follow hard the desperado's trail.
His threatened rifle stays us not, he finds no hope remains,
And yields at last a captive to, The Riders of the Plains.

We've taken haughty feathered chief, whose hands are red with blood;
E'en in the very council lodge, we seized him where he stood;
Three fearless hearts faced forty braves, and bore their chief in chains
Full sixty miles to where they camped, The Riders of the Plains.

But that which tries the courage sore, of horsemen and of steed
Is want of blessed water, blessed water is our need
We'll face like men whate'er befalls, of perils, hardships, pains,
But God! Deny not water to, The Riders of the Plains.

We bear no uplifted banner, the soldier's care and pride;
No waving flag leads onward or horsemen as they ride.
Our only guide is duty's call; and well its strength sustains
The dauntless spirit of our men, The Riders of the Plains.

We muster but three hundred men, in all this great lone land
Which stretches o'er the continent, to where the Rockies stand.
But not one heart doth falter, no coward voice complains
That few, too few in numbers are, The Riders of the Plains.

In Britain's mighty nation, each man must take his stand;
Some guard her honoured flag at sea, some bear it well on land.
'Tis not our part to fight its foes; then what to us remains?
What duties does our sovereign give, The Riders of the Plains.

Our mission is to plant the reign, of Britain's freedom here;
Restrain the lawless savage and protect the pioneer.
And 'tis a proud and daring trust, to hold these vast domains,
With but three hundred mounted men, The Riders of the Plains.

And thus we mind not praise nor fame, in the struggle here alone,
To carry out good Britain's law, and when our task has been performed
And law and order reigns, and plant old England's throne.
The peaceful settlers long will bless, The Riders of the Plains.

But death who comes to all alike, has smitten us out here,
Filling our hearts with bitter grief, our eyes with manly tears.
Five times he drew his fatal bow, his hands no prayer restrains;
Five times his arrows sped among, The Riders of the Plains.

Hard by the Old Man's River, where freshest breezes blow,
Five grassy mounds lie side by side, five riders sleep below.
Neat palings close the sacred ground; no stranger's step profanes
Their sweet repose; and they sleep well, The Riders of the Plains.

There is no marble column, there is no graven stone
To blazon to a curious world the deeds they may have done;
But the prairie flower blows lightly there, and creeping wild rose trains
Its wealth of summer beauty o'er, Those Riders of the Plains.

Sleep on, sleep on, young wanderers, who died in this Far West,
No prancing steed will feel your hand, no trumpet break your rest.
Sleep, till the great Archangel shall burst Death's mortal chains,
And you hear the great "reveille," Ye Riders of the Plains.

The Mounted Police are a Dashing Corps

—Anonymous

Composed during the 1870s, this may be about the Great March West, or another long patrol. Fort Ellice was the site chosen from Ottawa for the first NWMP headquarters; it was located where the Qu'Appelle River meets the Assiniboine. An old Hudson's Bay post, it proved unsuitable as a base for the western force. A site was then chosen at Fort Pelly, an old HBC post on the Swan River, not far from the aptly named Snake River; this post, in a remote, marshy area favoured by breeding snakes, served as base until it moved again to Fort Macleod in 1876. From Wake the Prairie Echoes.

Oh! The Mounted Police are a "dashing" Corps,
Though their horses are skinny and weary and sore.
Their sabres all shine in the morning light,
In wagons, where they are all boxed so tight.
And the sheen of the trappings glistens afar.
They are ready for rations, or water or war
I say they are ready, and there they remain,
But the rations are not, which is equally plain.
Though the wagons break down with the weight of the grub,
And sink in the mire, right up to the hub.
Our share of the grub is to guard it by day,
And go under arrest if a whisper we say.

Oh! What has become of the "Blarney" we heard,
As to how we'd be mounted and petted and cared.
Of the dashing career in store for us all,
Of the buffaloes shaggy we'd kill in the fall,
Of the Prairies Elysian we'd all march along,
Lulled sweetly to sleep by the nightingale's song.
Base, cruel deception, we live upon air,
At our ghoul-like appearance a convict would stare.
Of the buffaloes nothing remains but their skulls,
Which glare in the distance, like old shipwrecked hulls.
The absurd looking gopher is all that remains
Of all the vitality once on the plains.
Oh, give me some crackers, some pig or some beef,

Ye "Fort Ellice" heroes haste to our relief.
Our chargers are staggering over the plain,
Poor creatures are groaning with hunger and pain.
And we look like spectres all grimy and grim,
Oh, rise in your might and escort us all in.

The '74 Mounties

—Anonymous

This poem reminisces on the Great March West from the Red River almost to the Rockies. Originally from the Scarlet and Gold *magazine, it was reprinted in* Wake the Prairie Echoes.

Sixty-four years on the prairie, God but I'm growing old
I was just a lad in my teens, when I donned the Scarlet and Gold,
One of the North West Mounties. I have watched a city grow
On the banks of the Belly River, where I first saw the buffalo.

Sixty-four years on the prairie, it's hell how the time does fly
It seems like only a year or two since I bid the folks goodbye.
Striking west for adventure, maybe an Indian fray;
With a horse, a gun, and a saddle, plus my grub and four bits a day.

Sixty-four years on the prairie, boys, but the thought is grand
To have helped to make this province from the wild lone prairie land.
Still my heart yearns for the old days, with the Riders of the Plains.
And I'd like to be back in the saddle again, with my hands
        a-gripping the reins.

Ride On, Riders of the Plains

—Special-Constable R. Watkins-Pitchford

*The new Mounties created a colourful and proud impression as they came
riding through the town. This poem was written during the 1890s and is from*
RCMP Quarterly, *1935.*

> Ride on—ride on, riders of the plains,
> All the prancing horses are tugging at the reins,
> Hear the merry jingle, see the stirrups shine;
> Five-and-twenty cavaliers trotting into line.
>
> Ride on—ride on, riders of the King,
> Westward and eastward, riding with a swing,
> See the red coats flashing, jogging into rhyme,
> And a jaunty lot of Stetsons nodding to the time.
>
> Ride on—ride on, riders of the Crown,
> Listen to the cheering up and down the town.
> Riding with a swagger that tingles in your veins;
> They're for law and order, the riders of the plains.

The Trek of the NWMP

—Robert O. Kolke, Saskatoon, Saskatchewan

This poem was published by my late uncle, Robert Kolke, in his book Poems and Photographs *of the Canadian West. He grew up west of Estevan, Saskatchewan, where the Great March passed by the place his parents later homesteaded. Fort Dufferin to Roche Percée constituted the first segment of the long march. Scout Hill may refer to the "Hill of the Murdered Scout" in southern Manitoba, where a Cree is said to have battled a Sioux warrior to the death.*

> To Dufferin on our southern border,
> Came these men of law and order.
> To put an end to theft and murder;
> On the frontier stretching further.
> With machines and cattle and all gear;
> Far from all they once held dear;
> In that eighteen seventy-fourth year;
> Trekked the North West Mounted.
>
> It was hot and dusty summer weather;
> With smell of sweat and saddle leather,
> Cart wheels creaking all together;
> Crossed the valleys of the Souris River.
> Past Scout Hill's ancient burial ground;
> Then at the Indians' ceremonial ground;
> By Roche Percée they camped around;
> The men of the North West Mounted.
>
> Past where the woods no longer grow;
> Following Long Creek's stagnant flow;
> Where hot and gusty west winds blow;
> Lie the bleaching bones of buffalo.
> The trail is long, the days are dreary;
> When night is falling men are weary;
> Coyotes are howling, lonesome, eerie;
> On the Trek of the North West Mounties.

To dawn's bugle call the camp awakes;
Over rolling hills the morning breaks;
The winding trail the cavalcade takes;
Past deep valleys, white-rimmed lakes.
Where buffalo feed in morning light;
The deer and antelope take fright;
The Cypress Hills now come in sight;
Of the trekking North West Mounted.

Green were the hills, as an oasis;
Coniferous groves in sheltered places;
The hunting grounds of the Indian races;
Now men and beasts rest from their paces.
But gusty winds bring autumn chills;
They're driving beasts against their wills;
On toward the Sweet Grass Hills;
Trek the North West Mounties.

Snow on the prairie breezes tossing;
Past by the Belly River's crossing;
To where the Oldman River's washing;
There built a fort of logs and caulking.
To where the Oldman River's wending;
Mountains and the skies are blending;
There they reached their journey's ending;
The men of the North West Mounted.

Men of the Scarlet and Gold

—Margaret Moor, Red Deer, Alberta

This poem, written in the early 1900s, remembers Charcoal (Bad Young Man), who murdered another Native in southern Alberta because of a love affair gone wrong and subsequently murdered Sergeant Brock Wilde, who was pursuing him in a wild manhunt. Charcoal was executed in 1897.

> One night as I lay in the Valley of Dreams
> Far from my native shore;
> I was carried away on memory's wings,
> Back to the land of my youth once more.
>
> Till I stood on the top of a mountain height
> In the faraway Western Land;
> And saw in the shadow of long ago,
> The works of the Mighty Hand.
>
> I saw the great wide prairie stretch
> For a thousand miles and more;
> Where the Red Man hunted the buffalo herd,
> That roamed our plains in the days of yore.
>
> Away to the west where the Rockies stand
> And mountain torrents roar;
> And the lofty peaks of the Selkirk range,
> Roll down to the western shore.
>
> Then, lo, I saw a cavalcade—
> A strange white train;
> 'Twas the covered wagon, the prairie schooner,
> The ship of the western plain.
>
> Intrepid men of the early west,
> Pioneers of a great lone land;
> Braving the dangers they knew were theirs,
> A hoping, trusting, straggling band.

Then I turned and gazing away to the east,
Did a wondrous sight behold;
'Twas a body of men, a scanty few,
Clothed in colours of Scarlet and Gold.

No glory, no pomp, no welcoming band,
To greet those riders of old;
No generous board or downy couch,
Awaited our men of the Scarlet and Gold.

Should night o'ertake them as they rode,
Those men of the long patrol;
Their downy couch, the virgin sod,
Their pillow, a rising knoll.

What cared they for prowling wolves,
Or the wily Red Man's dart?
For beneath that tunic of scarlet serge
They carried a brave and fearless heart.

Swiftly now the leaves I turn
And strange new scenes I meet;
Settlers' homes, herds of cattle,
And fields of waving golden wheat.

And out on the open prairie wide,
In summer's heat and winter's cold;
The settler sleeps without a fear
Guarded by men of the Scarlet and Gold.

I turn a page in the Book of Time,
And memory's leaves unfold;
Then I see in my vision a sacred spot
Where sleep five riders of the Scarlet and Gold.

Five times the Red Man drew his bow,
And swift the arrow sped;
Five grassy mounds lay side by side,
There sleep our honoured dead.

And once again on the windswept plain,
'Neath the blazing scorching sun;
Lay a form so still, riddled and torn,
A victim of Charcoal's deadly gun.

Sleep on, young slumberers, take your rest
Members of that gallant band;
Who blazed the trail and scoured the plains,
And carried the law through the great lone land.

They need no marble column,
Carved in letters of gold,
To tell to this curious world of ours,
Deeds that were done by those riders of old.

The dangers and trials, hardships and perils,
Their dauntless courage and noble career
Are stamped forever with love and pride,
On the grateful heart of the Pioneer.

Oh, would that my pen could forever go on
In honest endless praise;
And tell of the glorious deeds that were done,
By the Scarlet Riders of pioneer days.

Honour their memory, think of them kindly,
Men of a thousand trails of old;
Who guarded the west in the days of unrest,
Dauntless men of the Scarlet and Gold.

The Scarlet Riders

—J.G. Wilson

From Lightfoot, Lord of the Mighty Pack and Other Poems. *There is no publication information on this book, but I suspect it was published a very long time ago.*

Who are the men that are passing
With the roll of the countless age,
That are known from the frozen Arctic
South to the purple sage.
The men that have stood for justice
Thro' Canada's vast domains—
These men are the scarlet riders,
The riders of the plains.

South where the rolling prairies
Rise up to meet the sky,
They rode in the wake of the sage brush
To the tune of the buzzard's cry.
Hard riding the trail of the outlaw,
There under the scorching sun,
They rode to the lair of the bandits,
Bringing to justice each one.

They were feared by the toughest criminal,
For oft times, stories were told
Of deeds that were done by these riders,
So fearless, courageous, and bold.
That the rules of their little red manual
Were so in their minds impressed,
That they got each man they went after
Tho' he were of the devil possessed.

In the first mad rush to the Yukon,
Where crowds did surge and roll,
They enforced there the law and its order,
In the shadows of the Pole.

They braved in winter its blizzards
In summer its storms and rains,
Just as true to their little red manual
As their comrades on the plains.

When the deeds of the nation's heroes
Are pressed in its history book,
You may look through its countless pages
And find there in every nook,
Deeds that are set down as valour
With a list of its heroes' names,
You will find there the scarlet riders—
The Riders of the Plains.

The Rustler's Lament

—Constable Ralph S. Kendall, #4351

From Constable Kendall's 1918 book Benton of the Royal Mounted *(Grosset and Dunlap, New York). The culprit outsmarted the American lawmen, but was caught by the Mounted Police.*

"Oh, Sheriff an' ranger both wished me luck,
Yu' bet! when I jumped th' Line last fall,
Yep! … Kind that a hog gets when he's stuck,
For I'd cert'nly made them cattle-men bawl.

Them fellers has cause to love me as much,
As they do a wolf, or a sneakin' Piute;
But wouldn't this jar yu'—gettin' in 'Dutch'
With th' Mounted Police, thru' a mangy coyote."

The RCMP

—S.W. Skilling, Calgary, Alberta

From RCMP Quarterly, *1942.*

Part of the West that will never die, but will live in the human ken
As a body that's ever fair and just, unspoiled by the greed of men.

Founded on little but courage and youth, they asked neither riches nor
    gain,
But set for themselves an honour code; an ideal they still keep in their
    name.

To that ideal they clung in the early years, though they suffered hardships
    and pain,
Faced death, or died, but they helped to build a force that's won worldwide
    fame.

Friend of the red man as well as the white, they proved when the West was
    young
That justice and mutual trust exchanged, were greater than sword or gun.

Part of the West that will never die, whatever the future may hold,
Respected by every race and creed, our men of the scarlet and gold.

The Lost Mounted Policeman

—John D. Higinbotham

Constable Charles Parker became known as "The Lost Mounted Policeman" in March 1883, when he and his horse Custer became lost in a snowstorm carrying a dispatch from the Blood Indian Reserve to the detachment on the St. Mary's River in Alberta. He was in a vast howling wilderness for a full week, frozen and famished. From Higinbotham's book When the West Was Young *(Ryerson Press, Toronto, 1933).*

"Say, Parker, 'tis a bitter day.
These March winds make one shiver;
Put saddle with what speed you may
And take this to the river.
And come and have a bite of food
Before you may go away.
For sure you'll need a good square meal
To keep the cold at bay.

"I willingly would go myself,
But do not know the road;
And travel is so bad just now,
I'd make too great a load.
But you are light, and young and strong,
With warm blood in your veins;
'Twill take the numbing cold a while
To make you drop the reins.

"So rustle now, my bonnie lad,
These days have little light,
And this dispatch must reach the camp
Before it comes on night."
Thus spake my Sergeant, and for me
'Twas only to obey;
But well I knew what risk I ran
In going out that day.

The hurried dinner soon was o'er,
And Custer had his feed;
And having put the saddle on,
I mounted on my steed.
Adieus all said, away we sped,
As fast as we could go;
But winds from off the Rockies' side
Had filled the trail with snow.

Well, on we plodded, and the trail
I patiently did seek,
Until at last I saw ahead
A welcome sight, Lee's Creek.
Soon I will reach St. Mary's brink;
It can't be very long
Before I see my comrades' fire,
And hear their merry song.

No shipwreck'd seaman, far from shore,
And 'neath an angry sky,
Could have less hope of being saved,
Nor suffer more than I;
My throat all parched from eating snow,
Face blister'd with the sun,
Hungry, half-frozen, blind and lost,
A helpless, hopeless one.

In fancy, I would sometimes see
A flock of grazing sheep,
And while I gazed, some famished wolves
Upon their necks would leap;
Again, I saw a smuggler's camp,
Which looked to me quite near;
But as I turned my horse that way
It seemed to disappear.

And then there came a pretty sight,
Which gave me comfort too.
I saw, in evening's light, the form
Of she I used to woo;
Fair as the sunny flowerets,
And lovely as the rose,
A heavenly smile lit up her face,
Which banished all my woes.

But oh, those joys were transient,
The dread reaction came;
I longed for death, or to be found,
To me 'twere all the same;
Day followed day, till six were past,
And still no help was nigh,
When in the snow, upon my knees,
I called to God on high.

My prayer was heard, an answer came,
God's mercies never fail,
For I could hear and faintly see,
The coming "Benton Mail."
When found, at last, my strength gave out,
Friends took me from my steed;
Kind helping hands were soon at work,
Supplying every need.

But ah, my lad, false hopes are thine,
The river you have crossed;
Out on the prairie's waste thou art,
And more than that—thou'rt lost.
On, on we went, till o'er us fell
The sable robes of night;
Watchful, but weary, down I lay,
And waited for the light.

I took the saddle blanket off,
And let poor Custer go;
Then up and down I tramped, to form
A coffin in the snow.
My ears were frozen, so I wrapt
The blanket round my head;
And taking one last look around,
I sought my snowy bed.

The wind was piping loud o'erhead,
The snow fell thick and fast;
The horrid howl of prairie wolves
Was borne upon the blast.
E'en with the howls of wind and wolves
Sweet slumber came to me;
I dream't of banquets, lordly feasts
And friends I ne'er would see.

The tempest passed, and morning's sun
Now shed its beams around;
And found me laid, in stately pomp,
Upon a narrow mound.
The ground was bare about my bed,
Custer stood at my feet,
For he had scraped the snow away
To get some grass to eat.

Tho' hungry still, we started out,
The long lost trail to find;
Naught but the snow was seen before,
And vast waste, behind;
The prairie looked so awful red,
Such strange thoughts crossed my mind,
These dreadful facts now made me feel
That I was struck snowblind.

When nearing Fort Macleod at last
I raised my head to see
My comrades gathered round the gate,
They cheer'd me lustily;
One day, when in the hospital,
Tho' only bones and skin,
They brought poor Custer to the door,
But could not bring him in.

"Come, Custer, come," I called aloud,
He neigh'd, then eyed the place;
And walking up to where I lay,
He gently licked my face.
"Ah, noblest of a faithful race,
The horse that brought me through,
If e'er I lose myself again,
I want a friend in you."

To Our Comrade

—Corporal W.W. Smith, #866

An unsung hero of the Force and Canada, Constable David Latimer Cowan, #635, from Ottawa, Ontario, was mutilated and killed by Natives on April 14, 1885, at Fort Pitt during the Saskatchewan Rebellion. He was buried by his comrades where he fell. From Scarlet and Gold *and* Wake The Prairie Echoes.

Farewell, young Comrade, the bleak northern plains
And frozen lakes shall ne'er know thee again,
No more swift Firefly again you'll e'er bestride,
The gallant roan fell by his master's side,
And ages hence, hist'ry shall count with pride
How for his Country, Cowan fought and died.
A horde of Painted Fiends on murder bent,
Maddened by blood from helpless victims rent,
Lined all the hill around.

Returning from a stern and perilous ride,
He marked the Indians, cached on every side,
Home sent the spurs into his charger's side
Right through their centre like a flash he rides,
He gains the hill, then 'neath his comrades' eyes,
Reels in his saddle, slowly falls and dies.

Oh, for a troop of his old Comrades there
His death had cost the painted savage dear,
Now 'tis all past and by Saskatchewan's stream.
The trooper's buried—softly may he dream.
Farewell old Comrade, sleep to wake no more,
'Till we meet at the Grand Reveille.

The Story of the Watch

—Hazel (Mrs. John) Lightle, Acton, Ontario

Written in 1975, this whimsical poem is based on a true story and features a famous connection. Wandering Spirit, who acquired the watch with a history, was a ruthless war chief at the time of the Northwest Rebellion. He was executed by hanging, along with seven others, in November 1885 at Battleford, Saskatchewan.

This gold watch has a history, it belonged beside a book,
The owner, writing stories, stopped sometimes to have a look.
One day, author Charles Dickens came to his Journey's End,
His third son became the owner of the watch, a faithful friend.
Soon across the broad Atlantic to the vast, wide prairie land,
Francis Dickens joined the Mounted Police, rode the prairies with this Band.

Inspector Dickens with his Mounties—twenty men and four,
At Fort Pitt were stationed, when the Métis went to war.
Wandering Spirit was the leader of the warriors of the Cree,
Their hearts were filled with rumours of Frog Lake's destiny.
Inspector Dickens' decision: to leave besieged Fort Pitt that day,
Be on the way to Battleford, more than a hundred miles away.

In a homemade leaking scow, they rode the rolling river,
The six-day hardships they endured, would set all hearts a-quiver.
The personal belongings of these men were left behind,
Inspector Dickens' watch the Indians did find.
Wandering Spirit took and wore it on his belt so long ago,
There it kept a-ticking as it was swinging to and fro.
Where Wandering Spirit wandered it was there by his side,
As the days of war lengthened, then came the turning of the tide.
Peace came to the prairies, and the Métis uprising o'er,
Inspector Dickens won his watch back at the closing of the war.

This story has an ending, this tale I've told is true,
A few of the details I have told them here to you.
Long years have gone swiftly, and the watch is here to stay,
A gentleman's proud owner of that watch from yesterday.

Cottonwood Coulee

—Hazel (Mrs. John) Lightle, Acton, Ontario

The NWMP headquarters were moved in 1878 from Fort Macleod to Fort Walsh in the Cypress Hills. From Scarlet and Gold, *Vancouver, 1976.*

South of Fort Walsh there's a coulee
Where the cottonwoods grow;
By the Cypress Hills o'er shadowed
And the sweeping west winds blow.

Through the Cottonwood Coulee
In the days of long ago;
Founding law and order
Mounted Police rode to and fro.

Maintaining right and justice
Until peaceful days were won;
Seven years the life span
The detachment's time run.

Vanished and silent the hoof beats
Only the legend remains;
Lost are the trails of the Coulee
Gone the Riders of the Plains.

In this quiet secluded coulee
The strangers seldom pass;
By a stone marker with its story
Hidden in luxuriant grass.

The Prairie Detachment

—Constable Ralph S. Kendall, #4351

Another poem by Ralph Kendall, this one reflecting on the mixed charms of an early Mountie's life on the Canadian frontier. From his book Benton of the Royal Mounted.

> And if you're wishful, oh maiden kind,
> To know concerning me;
> A far-flung sentinel am I,
> Of the RNWMP,
> Renouncing women, as though wearing a cowl.
>
> I live for a monthly wage,
> 'Way out on the bald, green-brown prairie,
> That stretches as far as the eye can see;
> Where the lone grey wolf and the coyote howl,
> And the badger digs in the sage.

The Ghost at the Barracks

—Henry Condie, Regina, Saskatchewan

Written in 1952, this spellbinding poem, eerily reminiscent of the ghost of Hamlet's murdered father, speaks of Louis Riel, who was hanged in November 1885 following the Saskatchewan Rebellion.

Midnight chimed on a clock somewhere,
And the young guard yawned and thought of his bed.
A windless night, with a nip in the air;
And the moon leered down on the barracks square.
A dying moon, blood-red.

The moon, could it speak, had a tale to tell,
A grisly tale, all grim and sad,
For this was the day they had hanged Riel;
From here they sent the poor breed to hell.
Better watch out, my lad.

The goose flesh pricked in the young guard's hair,
And he rubbed his brow and said, "What the hell!"
He looked over his shoulder across the square
With the small boy's fear that something was there!
"Nuts!" he said. "Nuts to Riel!"

The young guard scoffed, but into his head,
Came forgotten thoughts of the rebel chief,
Conflicting tales he had heard and read,
Of the tortured mind of a man crossbred,
A soul foredoomed to grief.

A passionate breed with a Roman's head,
A scholarly man with Indian blood,
Whose heart, where divergent virtues wed,
Would follow blindly where passion led,
Though evil should be his good.

Rebel and murderer, Ottawa said;
By his half-breed kinsmen, a hero hailed.
He had challenged an empire and made his bed,
To moulder with time's dishonoured dead,
The fate of the men who failed.

A rebel twice in a short life span!
It had taken guts, with the odds so great.
Each fight had been lost before it began,
But a hopeless flight was the mark of a man;
Only heroes challenge fate.

His wards had laid the tomahawk down;
How had they fared as the victor's wards?
Dragged out at fairs and parades to clown;
Kings of a continent wearing a crown
Made of junk from their broken shards.

Their chiefs could have taught our statesmen their craft;
Their braves coached the Mounties to ride a horse;
The young guard threw back his head and laughed,
If they heard this stuff they would say he was daft
And kick him out of the force.

Was the Cause lost and no more to be said?
If Truth was the daughter of Time she was late,
For the men who had played the big parts were dead.
The young guard shook the sleep from his head
And leaned hard on the gate.

He leaned on the gate and looked into the square
Where the red moon shone like a spotlight from hell.
And the young guard felt the stir in his hair
As a form took shape in the moonlit air,
A form he knew—Riel!

Tall and wide-shouldered, the Roman's head,
The scholar's brow, the luxuriant hair;
Queer burning eyes for a man who was dead!
(Yet not so queer when he'd Hell for a bed)
Not Riel but his ghost stood there!

Alert but in doubt the young guard stood,
He would do his job whatever the cost:
But to say "Who goes there?" would sound a bit crude.
Still challenge he must, did a stranger intrude;
But how did one challenge a ghost?

Then what? Surely here was such monstrous luck
As the strangest guard duty annals could boast;
A mad situation created by luck;
But one which the sentry was powerless to duck;
He felt somewhat peeved with the ghost.

He stood undecided in doubt and surprise.
Did the ghost guess why the sentry was mute?
For the fire died down in the burning eyes,
As the fire in the burnt-out embers dies,
And it raised a hand in salute.

The guard returned the salute and said:
"Why do you come here, Louis Riel?
Your people are happy, well housed, and well fed:
The land has known peace since the day you were dead,
What brings you back from hell?"

"The Truth is my answer," the ghost replied.
"The peace you speak of is worse than hell.
My people have lived like dogs since I died;
Chained to their kennels, in pain they have cried,
Come and feed us, Louis Riel!

"On their land they are herded like brutes in a pen,
The land they once owned from the sea to the sea.
Here where they hunted since time beyond ken,
All they ask is the chance to live like men,
The right to be equal and free.

"Wait! There is more and my time is fleet;
Consider this thing and my tale is done,
Think of the squaws and the red men you meet,
How they slink down the shady side of the street,
Afraid to look at the sun.

"With shoulders hunched and averted head,
They scuttle out of the white man's way.
Think now: of the braves who fought and bled,
Is the pride departed, the courage dead
That were theirs in a bygone day?

"These virtues still live; their blood is the same,
With patience teach them the white man's skill,
Make them forget their defeat and their shame,
Give back their manhood, in deed as in name!
In time you may work God's will."

The voice died and ghost dissolved in air.
The east was grey where the sun would rise.
The young guard's fingers rubbed his hair
As he vacantly gazed on the empty square,
A thoughtful look in his eyes.

Law and Order

—Anonymous

This poem recalls the lawlessness that followed railway construction in western Canada, as well as the role of the Mounties in combatting the unruliness of the times. Written circa 1919.

In the early days of the "Hobo" ranch, just west of Lac-St-Anne,
Before the rush of settlers, or the railway work began,
The Police of the North West Mounted and the Gunns of the Hudson's Bay
Were the only neighbours that we had that were surely there to stay.
Our cattle grazed for many miles, our horses roamed the hills,
The Police were never hampered, by reports of hidden stills.

But soon the word was passed around, the railroad's going west,
Old Peter Gunn was made "J.P." and tried the various cases,
The scum of foreign nations would be mingled with the best,
Of theft and crime, quite new to us, but old to alien races.
The Police they rode the lonely trails, loomed up like Phantom Ghosts,
They kept the law and order, in the camps of many hosts.

I knew them all, from first to last, the Police of Lac-St-Anne;
Now many of those boys are gone, to God's eternal clan,
Garrick, Baldy, Wilson, all now beyond the pale.
While Tyler is blind in London, the result of a German shell.
The "Hobo" boys are split and gone, Billy was killed in France,
John lives in California, while I'm in New York, by chance.
The Gunns have left the Hudson's Bay, Peter is Sheriff up there I think,
Where he keeps law and order on Strathcona's curling rink.

Going to Banff

—Constable. Cecil E. Morgan, #1749, Brantford, Ontario

This humorous poem, written in 1934, is likely based on fact. Superintendent John H. McIllree was one of the originals of the Great March; his regimental number was six. He commanded "E" Division, Calgary, Alberta, when Banff detachment was established as an outpost in 1886.

This is the story of Corporal D.
Who was sent to Banff along o' me
By Superintendent McIllree.

The Railway Station at Banff was a shack
Where we'd drop off a train, then take the next back,
Until Brett made a kick that his tax honorarium
Should furnish Police for his new Sanatorium,
So they sent a detachment of Corporal D.,
A splendid policeman, and strictly T.T.,
Two bronks with two saddles and Constable—Me.
'Twas in the winter of '86
That D. and I got into a fix
In a dark boxcar of frozen pig
With two mad bronks (and one a rig)
The meanest beast I've ever seen,
D.'s was tame but mine was green,
But we shoved 'em in, with squeals and jigs,
That cold boxcar half-filled with pigs.

We tied them short and we did our best
With hay and blankets to make a nest
For the long cold trip up the Rockies' rise,
Then dozed—but, it seemed, scarce closed our eyes,
When a clank of chain and a dropping pin
Conveyed the news that they'd locked us in

And ere we could yell or shout or grunt,
Kerflunk—banged an engine—we'd started to shunt
At the first concuss my bronk broke loose
And with teeth and heels played the very deuce
And D.'s old grey you can hardly blame
For breaking his halter and joining the game.

We roared for help as we took the points
With a jolt that quivered in all our joints
And I swallowed a chew that I should have spit
When a hoof caught my pants on the place where I sit
And then how I did it I don't know now
For it's very much lighter inside of a cow,
But I climbed up the pigs that were nearest to me
And there on the top I met Corporal D.
"Go tie up those horses," he said, "or you'll rue,
If you fail to obey me." I said, "You tie too?"
So we called an armistice and perched on the pork,
We adjured bronks forever—in future we'd walk.

We stayed on the pigs where the roars, kicks and squeals,
In the darkness below told us how a chap feels
When he's dragged in by chains while a potentate feasts
And views others' remains down amongst the wild beasts.
So we sat on the pork, for our howls were in vain,
'Till some cowpunchers heard as we stopped at Cochrane.
They were really great chaps, though they chafed us, you know,
As they roped the foul fiends that were raging below,
Gave us rum and hot coffee, but sometimes I feel,
That as D. was teetotal he got a raw deal.

And thus it occurred as I've told it to you
How we didn't ride herd on those bronks, but it's true,
That Banff's first Detachment consisted of me,
Two bronks in a boxcar and Corporal D.

Early Song of the Barrack Room

—Anonymous

The chorus in this poem seems to contain a mix of English and some other unknown language. From RCMP Quarterly, *1942, and* Wake the Prairie Echoes.

Being out of work while down below,
I had no other place to go;
Friends and pals not on the increase
So I went and joined the Mounted Police.
We shipped on board the CPR,
Each one thanking his lucky star,
The medical test successfully passed,
Each with a government job at last.

Chorus: Come on and join the Shemagonish outfit,
It's a mistake soneyas pay.
Get neyaninosap ta twabisk a month,
That's just fifty cents a day.

At Regina we arrived one noon,
And learned to use the shovel and broom;
Then they hustled us out upon the square,
The balance or goosestep to prepare.
'Twould curdle the milk in any churn
To hear Pat Mahoney's "Right about turn,"
And "Point your toes, hold up your head."
Till all the men wished they were dead

At the riding school we fared as bad;
Without the saddles we wished we had,
While veterans looked on with satisfied sneer,
To see some coyote pitched on his ear.
We'd ride a bronco that would buck and jump,
With a shoulder stick set to straighten our hump,
The boys all shouted, "Stay with him, Pat,
Get on that coyote, I'll hold your hat."

A Life in a Wooden Shack

—George E. Grogan, #459

Sung to the tune of "A Life on the Ocean Wave," by Epes Sargent. Singing was a vital component of entertainment and a great morale booster.

A life in a wooden shack, when the rain begins to fall,
Drip, drip thro' holes in the roof, and zephyrs come through the wall.
The tenderfoot curses his luck, and sighs out feebly,
"Ah, the blooming country's a fraud, and I want to go home to Mamma."

Chorus: Yah, Yah. I want to go home to Mamma.
        Yah, Bah. I want to go home to Mamma.

Intending to start him a fire when it's forty below;
He aims to chop at a log, and amputates his toe.
He hobbles back to his shack, and sighs out feebly,
"Ah, the blooming country's a fraud, and I want to go home to Mamma."

He saddles the fiery cayuse, intending to flourish around;
But the buzzard starts to buck, and lays him out on the ground.
He picks himself up with a curse, and sighs out feebly,
"Ah, the blooming country's a fraud, and I want to go home to Mamma."

He buys all the lots he can at the wrong end of Calgary;
And waits and waits for the "Boom" until he's dead broke like me.
So he has to exist on "tick" and sighs out feebly,
"Ah, the blooming country's a fraud, and I want to go home to Mamma."

He cannot get any work, and he wouldn't know how if he could;
So they run him in for a "vag" and set him to bucking wood.
He sits in the Guard room cell, and sighs out feebly,
"Ah, the blooming country's a fraud, and I want to go home to Mamma."

Now all ye tenderfeet list, before ye travel so far;
If you can't get a government sit, you'd better stay where you are.
Then you'll never be out of luck, and sigh out feebly,
"Ah, the blooming country's a fraud, and I want to go home to Mamma."

Pass the Tea

—Frank Carruthers, #282A

Another humorous ditty, sung to the tune of "Kingdom Coming," by Henry C. Work.

> Say, tenderfoot, you have seen us Mounties,
> We're a tough and hardboiled set.
> We're a terror to all evil doers.
> For we grab them quick—you bet.
> To horse thieves we have grown so partial
> We invite them home to stay.
> And with every other low offender
> We are bound to do away.
>
> Chorus: Then pass the tea, and let us drink,
>   We guardians of the land.
>   You bet your life it's not our fault,
>   That whiskey's contraband.
>
> We "buck" sometimes, and grouch a little
> When there's "Mud Fatigue" to do;
> But when duty calls us to the saddle
> Our hearts are brave and true.
> We like our duty and we do it
> The right for to maintain.
> When rides are long, and "grub pile" short,
> We Mounties don't complain.
>
> When we hit the trail in hot pursuit
> Of hostile Cree or Sioux,
> The feathered Chieftain hurls this curse
> Nah-mow-yah ran-oo-kan-boo.
> So don't get hostile if you find
> Five aces in our hand;
> For sometimes we must "stack" the cards
> To keep order in the land.

HUNTERS AND WARRIORS

Obituary to the Nitche

—Corporal D.A. Fleming, #6095

"He asked for but a hunting ground, and foes to win him fame" are stirring words. The author composed this poem circa 1890, while stationed at Wood Mountain in southern Saskatchewan. Whether the Nitche is the name of a real or fictitious tribe is unknown and probably not that important, as the poem seems to mourn the universal passing of the time-honoured traditions and way of life that belonged to all the Native peoples of the North American west.

The western winds sweep quietly
O'er the sleeping plains so still,
And bend the guardian cactus
And sage on draw and hill.

Soft mumbling from the creek bed,
Soft murmuring from the grass,
While tumbleweed goes sweeping
For things, now of the past.

A requiem set by Nature
To mourn the Indian brave,
Who sleeps beneath the prairie
On his forgotten grave.

No more the Shaganappi thong
Shall his war lance adorn;
And mouldered are his tepee poles
By circle stones forlorn.

His bow forever vanished,
That foe-ward hissing sent
The sight of death—the arrow,
Its flight forever spent.

The moccasins of smoke-tan,
That stilled his stealthy tread,
No more will bear his supple form
O'er draw and river bed.

The war club of grey granite,
The bow cord of elk gut—
They earned for him the right to step
The war dance boasting strut.

No soft-ribbed code he sponsored
To lull his warrior heart.
His honour was to laugh at Death
When he had played his part.

He asked for but a hunting ground;
And foes to win him fame,
And fortitude to meet his end
By arrow, knife or flame.

To live in life—Valhalla,
Come death—the hunt and chase,
In Happy Hunting Grounds beyond
The outer rim of space.

While western winds tell softly
Of days that used to be,
Sleep on, you knight of Nature,
Your spirit still is free.

The Skull

—Constable W.H. Mitchell, #1143

Musings on an Indian skull unearthed on the bank of Long Creek, west of Estevan, Saskatchewan. Written circa 1893.

In a lone grave on Long Creek bank
'Neath a rude mound of stone,
Up reared by kin—with loving toil
This Indian skull was found.

Long years have rolled their weary rounds
Since first the setting sun
Cheered this lone grave with lingering ray
Then sank 'neath the western dome.

The bison oft the grass hath cropped
Around this sacred spot
Or rushing o'er with thundering tread
His slumbers wakened not.

Dakota's thunder claps might peal
The cyclone spends its might
And lightning lurid flash illume
The murkiest gloom of night.

Unmindful still, he slumbered on
This Red Man of the plains
Nor storm, nor war whoops' fierce alarm
Stirred his dull ear again.

Oft did he stroll those banks along
In halcyon days gone by
When Red Man ruled these mighty plains
Unbounded, save by sky.

When bison herds in sweet content
By thousands grazed around
Darkening the plains with shaggy forms
Wide as horizons bound.

When stately elk, with ponderous horns
In Long Creek vale hard by
Slow sauntered through the leafy glade
Unseen by white man's eye.

When oft along yon winding stream
Mid vales bedecked with leaves
Unharmed as in their pristine days
Contented beaver lived.

A Ballad of the West

—George E. White, #3574

*Sir George French was the first commissioner of the Force and commanded
the Great March West. Written circa 1900, this poem tells a great story of the
early police days. Fort Whoop-up was one of several lawless whiskey-trading
posts in the area north of Montana. Jerry Potts was a Métis guide who led the
NWMP to the Oldman River in 1874.*

All ye who, astraddle a Western stock saddle,
Have loped through the foothills and over the plain,
In fancy ride with me, down trails of past hist'ry;
And join in the deeds of the old Force again.

These prairies and hills, these coulees and rills,
Saw many a Blackfoot and Plain Cree foray.
In all this land over, to each red-skinned rover,
The law of survival, by fighting, held sway.

Then in came the "Paleface" with whiskey and "Squareface,"
The Indian's body and soul not his own.
Once tasting "firewater," hides, horse, squaw or daughter
He'd swap for liquor that ravaged his home.

Along the wide border was no law or order,
The Red Man debased by the bootlegger's sway.
Unprincipled trader and "Fort Whoop-up raider,"
The Montana "Long-knives" were lords of the day.

'Mid orgies and mysteries, there were wailings and miseries;
Bloodlust and hatred were thereby revived.
But, at this crucial moment, with chaos in foment,
Commissioner French and his Mounted arrived.

Each Indian brother heard the great white Queen Mother
Had decided to offer forbearance and truth;
With Whoop-up demolished, and liquor abolished,
"Fair Play" proved the watchword, not "tooth for a tooth."

"Jim" Macleod, "Atty" Irvine (right down to the herdsman)
Jerry Potts, Nigger Annie, each and every stout heart,
Swung to the role, of aligning the whole
Of the "Wild Woolly West" to Canada's part.

For the Indian's weal—Walsh, Wood, Crozier, Steele,
Held fast to their motto of "Maintain the Right."
The Premier, Sir John, from the far east looked on,
Envisioned the coming of Dawn after Night.

Loomed the homestead and ranch rising quick to the chance
That gave homes and work to the man from afar.
With the New West's renown, came hamlet and town
Along the steel trail of the great CPR.

New ways had enveloped, until there developed
The open Rebellion in the year eighty-five.
Bad omens spread forth from Batoche in the north
Massacre at Frog Lake! Seemed no white could survive.

To arms and to horse, went the cry to the Force,
To Middleton's army they held the torch high.
Dumont and his Breeds, at Duck Lake, in sore needs—
To knock out the white man, they'd win, or they'd die.

Big Bear, the low-schemer; White Cap, the redeemer;
Poundmaker, the stout-hearted—the best of them all;
Wily Chief, plotting half-breed, base conniver of misdeed,
Strove vainly to conquer in one sweeping call.

On hand where most wanted, foe-facing, undaunted,
The Force in full confidence rode to the fight.
Then Riel was defeated; his forces retreated—
Dispersed when they fronted the plains Riders' might.

Rest ye your ghost horse, by the trail of the old Force
That runs through our memory without any stain.
By the beacons of glory, that dot all their story
We'll rest, for the present, then ride on again.

Letitia

—Robert O. Kolke, Saskatoon, Saskatchewan

Another poem by Robert Kolke, from his book Poems and Photographs of the Canadian West. *Written circa 1990.*

Letitia was Mac the white trader's daughter,
Her mother was a Swampy Cree.
She was more beautiful than the flowers,
And her spirit gay and free.

She said she would wed only a white man,
Not for her the lodge or tepee.
Though whites were few and not trustworthy
Yet not for her a Swampy Cree.

And so she made plans to catch this Mountie,
Not knowing that he had a fiancée
That was far away in an eastern province,
There was no one that she could see.

Then one day she made her way to their cabin,
When his pal was off and far away.
And there her wiles and charms she flaunted,
And led this lonely man astray.

From then on their meetings were so often,
And any chance together they would lay.
And she felt so sure that he would wed her,
Told him she'd have a child one day.

Then quickly he sent out an urgent message,
That he wished to be posted far away.
If he still planned to marry his fiancée,
At this place he could not stay.

Then he was posted to a northern outpost,
High up there among the Eskimo.
Where he was left to cool off his ardour,
Up there among the ice and snow.

Letitia now a sad and far wiser woman,
She went and lived among the Cree.
Her child grew up with Mac the trader,
As fine a lad as there could be.

The Near Battle of Cussed Creek

—Dr. T.A. Patrick, Yorkton, Saskatchewan

Written in 1894, this poem describes a volatile situation that occurred some seven years earlier, when the Natives under Chief Little Bones in the Yorkton area went on a marauding expedition among the settlements, slaughtering oxen, stealing horses, and looting houses. They demanded provisions and held war dances. Some of the terms used in this poem are a reflection of those tense, turbulent times. From former legislative librarian John Hawkes' book The Story of Saskatchewan and its People, Volume 1 *(Chicago, The S.J. Clarke Publishing Co., 1924).*

I went one night to an old fort's site,
Not far from Yorkton town;
And having the time, to make me a rhyme,
On its ramparts, sat me down.

There, much decayed, was the old stockade,
With its breastworks of prairie sod,
Where the Yorkton Guard, having laboured hard,
With martial footsteps, trod.

Inside was the well, which, truth to tell,
Was nothing like that at Cawnpore,
For none of the slain, were into it lain,
Nor crimsoned its waters with gore.

Close by was the ground, where their campfire around,
The Indians, with war whoop and yell,
Thought to frighten the Guard, by howling as hard,
As incarnate demons of hell.

There, the young Pepeech, with an imp-like screech,
 Fired off his smooth-bore gun,
 And old Little Bones, in hoarser tones,
 Out-bellowed his warlike son.

I saw the old mill; it was standing there still,
To which fled non-combatant whites;
Where they spent those dread days, in a fearful amaze;
Not to mention those terrible nights.

Where day after day, in fell dread wore away
Till "Big Sunday," the Major, took heart;
And sent out the scouts, not with noises and shouts;
But to play a white warrior's part.

In the grey of the dawn, these brave fellows marched on,
With their Sniders all loaded and primed;
Till they neared some tepees, hid themselves 'mong some trees;
And saw their advance was well-timed.

For as the sun rose, o'er the camp of their foes,
They saw not the blue smoke ascend
From the tepees' brown tops, for the braves were not up,
And but huskies the tepees defend.

But with the first growl, of these dogs came a howl,
From each warrior, and papoose, and squaw,
And they rushed to their arms, with the wildest alarms,
As two Sergeants advancing, they saw.

Now these Sergeants advanced, not on chargers that pranced,
But on foot, bravely facing the foe;
Each with jargon and sign, making known their design,
To bring peace, and not war, you must know.

But the squaws were the worst, of these demons accurst,
With the spirit of war and of woe,
For they would have shot those two men on the spot,
And they aimed with the arrow and bow.

The boys in the bluff, feeling then sure enough,
Their Sergeants were victims of war,
As they peered through the leaves, trained their guns on the braves,
And awaited the signal to fire.

"Forward march to the tents," and to give no offence,
"Ground your arms," said a Sergeant,
Who had he but sense, would have seen that defence,
Was a matter still urgent.

But those brave volunteers, with a valour that cheers,
Obeyed that stern duty and forward did go;
Placed their arms to the ground, looked then calmly around,
And returned with indifference, the gaze of the foe.

Their valour upbore them, the foe quailed before them.
He folded his tents and went, sullen, away;
And though time has wrought changes, on these western ranges,
That scene is recalled with a shudder today.

For even a stranger, will notice the danger,
Besetting these men, with their guns to the ground,
Had the redskins been bolder, their guns at the shoulder,
Four-and-twenty scalped corpses, some day had been found.

Old Little Bones lies, where mosquitoes and flies,
Are not likely to trouble him more.
And Welbury's dead, of whom truly 'twas said,
That he might have been shot in that war.

And as to the grave, Indian warriors who gave,
Indirectly, war medals, broadcast;
They can't be made white, in a day and a night;
And they'll all be "good Indians" at last.

And as to the men, they are scattered again,
To the north and the south, west and east;
And it can't be gainsaid, that though none were shot dead,
Quite a few have been half-shot at least.

To the oxen were slain, in this dreadful campaign,
No monuments rise at the fort.
So let it be said, that those oxen are dead,
And their tale, like this, is cut short.

The Hunter from Sixty Below

—Constable John W. Glover, #9707, Ross River, Yukon Territory

Based on a true story of the desperate need for food. Billy Cho (Diamond) was a great Native hunter; "Sixty Below" was the name of the flats below Ross River, where Constable Glover was stationed. Written in 1925.

It was on the eve of May twenty-fourth
When the rescue was made by comrade in force,
Footsteps approached, we sprang to the door,
Packed with fur stood old Diamond of yore.

"Moose!" cried the hunter from Sixty Below
He was on Mission flat not one hour ago.
"Gosh," said the host, "the bacon is low,
We must kill him, weather or no."

"I'm hungry," cried the hunter, "let me eat for a while
Of the beans on the table you so freshly boiled."
He kicked at the bacon—none could be found,
"No wonder," cried the host, the last time around.

So we put on our mufflers, our moccasins I mean,
And crept down the bank to search the ravine.
The willows not blooming, the spruce very low,
We squatted on the hilltop watching objects below.

Not a sound could be heard but a twit-twit-bub-bub,
"I see him," said the hunter, "in a thicket of shrub,
It is just a last-year's, toe-head scrub."
Then the starers cried, "Kill him, and be bold,
We will wait here until the liver is cold."

From the mightiest of men that noble hunter descended,
And into that thicket is he.
We heard but one shot—he cried from the spot:
"Fresh meat, follow me!"

The boast of this hunter, the pride of Sixty Below,
Who descended from hunters with arrow and bow,
And is known in Pelly as our Billy Cho.

THE ARCTIC

The Lost Patrol

—A. Glenn Broder

The four-man dog-sled patrol headed by Inspector F.J. Fitzgerald during the winter of 1910–11 between Fort MacPherson and Dawson, Yukon Territory, met a tragic end. The patrol annually carried mail, reports, and requisitions for supplies, but this particular expedition never reached its destination: all tragically starved and froze to death in the brutal Arctic weather. From the London Daily Mail, *March 1912, and* Wake the Prairie Echoes.

Mourn long, mourn deep, but shed no transient tear
For those who perished on the lonely trail
The untracked path of duty; craven fear
Nor laggard will e'er cause those hearts to quail
That now are still in death. Rather, lift up
In noble joy the head, that such as they,
Heroic, one by one, had drained the icy cup
With pallid lips, then passed the trackless way,
Brave spirits purified, while snow-enshrined there lay
The wasted forms that stay, so still, so still!

Though never may they reach their Northern goal,
Though lost the clue, though rash the unplanned guest,
They failed for lack of fear, each dauntless soul
At duty's call or Empire's bold behest
Unknown, unpraised, a thousand risks had run,
Taken wild chances, some good end to gain,
Counting success as naught; life's setting sun
Illuming with peace their path of pain
Crowned their unfinished task on frozen plain
With honour, not in vain, they lie so low, so low.

And he, their leader, chosen with the best
To hail the crowning of the King, went forth
Upon the distant trail to be the guest
Of death, pale-panoplied; the icy North
No purple splendour spread, nor pomp, nor state;

A solitary sentry at death's gate.
No cheering crowds acclaimed the path he trod;
As royal escort, lonely he must wait
At the last post the summons of his God,
And on the frigid sod, lie so still, so still.

Strong to endure, a leader to the last,
While yet he lingered on life's shadowy verge
What tender visions thro' his memory passed
Of all that made life sweet, no dreary dirge
Wailed in the ears of one so true to love
Of home and her who bore him duty done
Ere yet the life immortal had begun,
The northern lights in glory shone above,
Like messengers of heaven, to meet the one
Whose course on earth had run, so swiftly, yet so slow.

Mourn for the lost patrol who now no more,
On errands speed o'er foothill, gorge, and plain,
Wise in all trail and mountain lore,
On the long chase, or when thro' every vein.
The wind, with keen, cool sting had warmed the blood
And set the heart aglow, on charger fleet
They tireless rode and swam the mountain flood,
Or proudly paced a royal guest to meet.
Alas! These to whom action was so sweet
Here at our feet lie, so still, so still.

Slow falls the snow in deadly silence down,
And hard'ning hides the bare arid ground,
Where, desolate, afar from camp or town,
Gaunt woods, and spectral trees, weird shapes around
Stand motionless, unstirred by kindly breeze,
In the grim grasp of frost. Though bleak and drear,
The temple of the infinite is here.
Let us give thanks to God that such as these
The sacramental cup drank to the lees,
Here on our knees; then let us softly go.

Tribute to Inspector Fitzgerald and his Noble Band

—C. Burbidge, Calgary, Alberta

Another tribute to the lost patrol. From Wake the Prairie Echoes.

We have praises sung of soldiers and of sailors who have been
To fight in foreign places for their country, king and queen.
We've erected grand memorials to our heroes one by one,
But nothing for the gallant deeds our Mounted Police have done.

They've toiled for king and country in a most unceasing way.
They've civilized the Golden West, for next to nought in pay.
They've ridden out to lands unknown, these mounted heroes bold.
They've penetrated far, far north and perished in the cold.

So when you write your heroes down, you know of in this land,
Remember poor Fitzgerald and his gallant little band;
They went up north for duty into barren lands and shores
They suffered, starved, and gave their lives, all for our country's cause.

Just Mounted Police, those gallant souls, whose country is their pride;
'Twas for their country's cause Fitzgerald's men went out and died.
Erect a fine memorial for these men lest we forget,
They toiled for us, and on it have each hero's name inset.

Above place this inscription, so that all may understand:
"To the memory of Fitzgerald and his gallant little band
Who died on duty in that bitter frozen north so grim,
Called up to take a well earned rest above the skies with Him."

Duty

—F.G. Roe, Edmonton, Alberta

Another perspective on the heroes of the lost patrol. From RCMP *Quarterly, 1937.*

"It is supposed that the guide lost his bearings."
The guide stopped short in bitter black despair;
The storm-lashed leafless branches moaned and tossed;
The snow-dust swirled; then, "God!"—half curse, half prayer—
They heard his muttered sob of anguish—"Lost!"
And at the word their hearts within them died,
As brave men likewise have been known to sink;
And then the tonic of his native pride
Came back to brace them—"Wait, boys; let me think."
A week before ... or was it but a week? ...
They left that cruel God-forsaken stream ...
Two days ... it was two days ... they kept the creek
Toward the height of land ... it seemed a dream ...
And then ... O God! have mercy ... he recalled ...
Two creeks bore upward ... had he made a slip? ...
Was this the right one?—Petrified, appalled,
He strove to search his memories of the trip.

The one he knew ... or thought he knew ... and still? ...
That blinding storm ... it numbed one's very frame! ...
He'd swear he recognized that cut-bank hill ...
And yet ... that coulee didn't seem the same ...
"Two days along the creek," that half-breed said ...
"Then ... strike across toward the height of land."
But now ... three ... four ... five ... six ... a week had sped
Their weary traverse once again he scanned—
He'd heard of fellows turning 'round and 'round ...
He used to laugh ... and then ... the other day ...
He thought he knew that bit of scrubby ground ...
But even then? ... He hardly dared to say ...
They'd got the mail ... and mighty little grub ...
(He'd give them both for one good thorough warm)

They might as well camp down among the scrub
As waste their strength in that infernal storm ...
And who dare hope to picture, who may know,
What time the Storm-King's furies roared and mocked,
The horrors of that death-camp in the snow,
The hopes now shattered and again restored!

Those fruitless days of struggle, pain, and stress,
Striving to think their senses judged aright;
Those formless wastes of tortured barrenness,
Those mad delusions of the Arctic night!
The stricken guide by fell remorse assailed;
His agony of soul, when fortune failed,
Who'd staked their all upon a cast—and lost!
The sickness that is born of hope deferred
Methinks accepted each his equal share;
Nor will I deem they spoke one single word
To make that burden harder yet to bear.

By This We Shall Remember Them

—Anonymous

A final tribute to Inspector Fitzgerald's lost patrol. From Wake the Prairie Echoes.

High on the barren peak it stands
A monument put there by loving hands,
It marks the heroism they did display
As they explored the Barren Lands that day.
A crude stone Cairn
What story could it tell,
Of men who left their home
And went through Hell.

They braved the bleak and lonely dark of Arctic night,
Lighted only by the Aurora Borealis light
What thoughts were in their hearts,
Those Scarlet-Coated men,
Of homes and loved ones
Never to be seen again.
'Tis only through their notes
Which they have left behind,
That we who now live on.

The Red Marine

—Corporal W.G. Kerr, #7685

Written during the 1930s, this poem is about the men and life aboard the famous schooner St. Roch. *Commanded by Sergeant Henry A. Larsen, the ship twice sailed the North West Passage through the Arctic in the 1940s and also circumnavigated the North American continent, the first ship to do so. Later, Larsen was my commanding officer in the eastern Arctic. From* RCMP Quarterly *and* Wake the Prairie Echoes.

His hair was not, his back was bent,
His eyes roved to and fro.
He drank his beer and burped a lot
And smelled of horse B.O.
He looked as Caesar might have looked
When saying "Et tu, Brute?"
As if the fates had smashed him down
And left him beat and mute.
Thus sat he in the tavern gay
And joined not in the cheer
A wreck of life and foundering fast,
Just scuttled by much beer.

From off the street with spring step
Came a youth so bright and fair;
And smilingly he looked around
To find a vacant chair.
The hop-inhalers filled the place
There seemed to be no room,
But, Ah! A chair he sees beside
That fugitive from a tomb.
The flotsam stopped his weaving head
To see what once he was,
A'mirrored in that happy lad,
All energy and buzz.

"Oh, join with me and have an ale,"
The lad said with a grin.
"It's sad for beer to be without;
Much better to be within."
"Why for your happiness, my lad?"
Asked he whose race was run.
The boy replied, "Ah! Life is sweet
And all the world is fun.
I'm in the Force of Riders Red
And now go gladly forth,
For I applied and got the nod
To serve up in the North."

The undertaker's "work-to-be"
Paled at the youth's reply
As if the woes of other days
Had risen 'fore his eyes.
A frantic clutch to grasp his ale,
A gulp—and it was gone
And then to save the pangs of thirst,
He drank the other one.
"Where in the North will you be sent?"
Cried he who was a crock;
And then did swoon as the youth replied,
"Aboard our boat—*St. Roch.*"

The lad's quick wit took in the scene—
The form across the tables;
And brought the derelict back to life
By loudly yelling "Stables!"
"Why do you grieve that I go North?"
He asked that poor beer-blotter;
"Perchance romance was once your goal
And in the North you sought her?
I know you once were in the Force;
Oh! It's not hard to tell,
For who but pensioned Mounties
Have that beer and equine smell?"

"You're right my lad, I once wore red,
So hearken unto me,
I am to turn you from that path
That leads to misery.
I too was once a lad like you
And sought the Arctic rim
Upon that boat—named for a Saint,
But hewed from Satan's limb.
'Twas years ago I stepped aboard
To sail the Arctic Sea;
The best of me went overboard,
The rest—that now is me.

"Nine other men (they then were men)
Were mustered for her crew,
And joyfully we left the south
And headed for the Blue.
We heaved and rolled in Northern seas,
Our stomachs rolled as well,
Which proved to one and all of us
What Newton didn't tell.
He said what's up must sure come down
And we, sick as a pup,
Had proof of what had once been down
Was quickly coming up.

"The cook was not as mother was,
We wished him quite a fate,
It was the first time I had seen
Halitosis on a plate.
I ran the engine, pulled the sail,
Slept not in wind and fog,
I've fished, cut ice, unloaded freight
And even kept the log.
I scraped and washed the heaving deck
And baked the daily bread.
I've cleaned the hold and pumped the bilge
And heaved the heavy lead.

"I've lived for days among the floes
I've dallied on a reef,
And prayed the prayers that once I knew
For fear we'd come to grief.
A hundred times, to save the boat,
We took the cargo out.
"Now put it back before it's wet,"
We'd hear old Henry shout.
In rain and snow we worked the freight
When once we reached the post,
And stubbed our toes and barked our shins
Upon the rocky coast.

"And then when winter cloaked the land,
We'd tie us to a bay,
And when the ice made prison walls
For months and months we'd stay.
A purgatory in wood it was,
A hell without the flame,
And when the Spring broke up the ice
We'd start the rounds again.
I can't go on," the wrecked one cried,
"To rake my sore-tried soul,
But I will mention one thing more
And then my tale is told.

"'Mad Trapper' was a character
From out the Arctic waste;
Perchance, my lad, you read of him
And of his month-long chase.
And of the desperate deeds he did,
His poor brain warped by hate
And how at last by rifle lead
He finally met his fate.
And now they seek to learn his life
And the place whereof he came
But all they found is what they knew:
That Johnson was his name.

"But I could ease the ceaseless quest
If I should care to talk,
For one place only breeds such men
And that's the boat, *St. Roch.*
But why should I bow down to them;
This secret still is mine,
'Mad Trapper' he was only one,
I knew another nine."

The youth, he staggered forth again,
With vim and vigour cruelly slain,
And seeking a place of like dismay
He thus to Headquarters made his way.
And though he's still in deep despair
He's just the same as others there.

Ballad of the *St. Roch*

—Marjorie Reigh

Another poem about the famed schooner. The St. Roch *is preserved at the Vancouver Maritime Museum in Vancouver, British Columbia. From* RCMP Quarterly, *1962.*

A battered schooner named *St. Roch*
Lay beside the grimy dock
In deep dejection;
For she was bound both fore and aft
A prisoner deprived the waft
Of wind's direction.

No "Keep Off" order on her deck
Designed to foil the rubberneck
Could I perceive;
So I nimbly hoist myself aboard
And the Nor'west Passage route explored
In make-believe.

I sensed the strength of her design
Saw tarr'd ropes stiff with Arctic brine
Her stalwart masts;
I heard the grinding crash of ice
As it trapped her in its deadly vise
With polar blasts.

Beset by clammy ice-born fogs
I caught the whimper of husky dogs
Unchained, they cowered.
I saw the cairn on lonely strand,
The resting place of French Chartrand
In solitude unflowered.

When cook Dad Parry called the men
For a mug of scalding coffee, then
I took a gulp,
But felt myself with horror pale
As we watched the ice floes crush a whale
To bloody pulp.

With the treacherous Passage safe behind
We sailed to meet East coast's mankind
Down Labrador.
I cast my adventurous dreams aside,
Invented a reason to see inside,
Unlatched the door.

The fo'castle wore a desolate look
With cabins and galley by crew forsook
But I sat down
In the little saloon now nearly bare
With Her Majesty's picture, wondrous fair
In Garter'd gown.

I longed to tell this gallant ship
How I valued our brief acquaintanceship
As I said farewell;
And though her future lies berthed ashore
I'm certain her Spirit will evermore
In the Arctic dwell.

Manhunt in the Arctic

—J. Robert Barrett

The famous story of the Mad Trapper of Rat River, who met his demise in
1932—but not before he led the Mounties on a chase that lasted over six weeks
in the fierce Arctic winter. A dramatic, still-fascinating classic. From RCMP
Quarterly, *1942 and 1967.*

The Arctic post loomed like a ghost, and ice-waves chilled the veins;
Like a thing alive the snowflake drive had whipped the window panes;
And God! But the wind was a demon blind screaming a devil's song,
Choking the breath and icy as death, hurling the storms along;
Pouring its wrath down the Arctic path, spouting the shrapnel snows;
Howling stark in the frozen dark, wailing a thousand woes;
Like driven shot from a juggernaut, it brought the blizzard's sting,
With talon grip it seemed to strip, and lash each living thing.

Out of this hell with a tale to tell, an Indian runner sped,
And he told of the fear of a trapper queer, who strung their traps
    o'erhead;
Who swung the might of his six-foot height, along their trapline runs,
And cursed the face of the Indian race, and cowed them with his guns.
There were few who knew the trapper bold, from whence, or why he'd
    come;
And no one asked, and no one told, and the trapper's lips were dumb;
And the eyes of the law that ever saw the merits and the flaws,
Were dark and dim as they looked at him, and wondered who he was.

His ways were lone and he kept to his own, and he acted "bushed" and
    "queer,"
And he turned his guns on the friendly ones who dared to venture near.
There were looting tales of trapline trails, where the wild Rat River rolled,
And the law of the land stretched out its hand with its men in scarlet and
    gold.
The trapper's home raised its snow-peaked dome—double-walled and
    grim,

You could see at a glance he took no chance of anyone capturing him;
No foot of ground that stood around, from his rifle shot was free
For loop-holes stared, and waiting, glared as if the walls could see.

Two Mounties sped from Arctic Red across the storming land,
And swift they strode to the queer abode, and loud was the law's
     command,
And bullets tore through the massive door, as the trapper's rifle rumbled,
And a parka hood was stained with blood, and a Mountie reeled and
     stumbled.
And horror-steeled, his comrade wheeled, in the glare of the trapper's
     gun,
Grasping his friend, he struck for the bend, of the wild Rat River's run;
The dog whip slashed and the huskies dashed, and raced for Aklavik Post,
And on the sleigh the trapper's prey lay silent as a ghost.

The power and awe of the thwarted law, swung swift to the manhunt trail,
And the trapper's name leaped into fame, from its place beyond the pale.
Through wind and snow at forty below, a posse ploughed all day,
Half-blind and cold they fought the hold that barred their forward way;
With lash and grip of husky whip, they drove their straining dogs,
Till they came to the height where day and night, in his loop-holed fort of
     logs,
The trapper thought his tangled thoughts, and stared at the law of the
     land,
And sullen heard the clear-cut word, that was the law's command.

His rifle roar on the river shore, was answer to his wrong,
With screeching hell of bursting shell, he opened his battle song.
The law retired, and charged and fired, and then retired again,
Till they knew full well no rifle shell could pierce the trapper's den.
Though crude bombs hurled just rocked the world, and shattered the
     massive door,
The trapper still kept up his shrill and whining-bullet war.
At last the law, retiring, saw their dwindling food supply,
And shells were few and the Mounties knew, they must come for another
     try.

But the trapper's lair was cold and bare, upon their grim return,
And the trail-wise crew could find no clue, no hint of where to turn.
A search began for the hunted man, where even the dog-teams crawl,
Where frozen creeks and craggy peaks, and crooked canyons sprawl;
Where men must crush through tangled brush, and trails were never
    known,
Where the trapper'd gone by day and dawn, and fought his way alone,
With a devil's goad he packed his load, no husky sled he had,
And 'twas often said in days ahead, 'twas proof that he was mad.

Grim days went by and at last on high, on a rock and brush plateau
They saw a rough-made barricade, and the trapper crouched in the snow.
Their quarry fell as a well-aimed shell opened the battle raid;
In the frozen day for hours he lay, behind the barricade.
Each grim-faced man of the law began to stalk for the final fight,
And swift as storm the leaping form of the trapper shot in sight;
And as he sprang his rifle sang, and rained a hail of death,
And a Mountie moaned and writhed and gasped his final mortal breath.

The Northland rose in wrathful throes, and sworn to the law of the Crown,
Went men afire with the staunch desire, to hunt the trapper down;
And overhead on wings there sped the veteran pilot, May
To carry supplies through storming skies, along the manhunt way.
The battle raid on the barricade had forced the trapper's flight,
And the trail he took had a hurried look, where it haunted the foothill
    height.
With never a rest the trapper prest, across the high divide,
And close behind the manhunt grind, came down the Yukon side.

More and more of trail-wise lore, the trapper used each day,
As he watched them fail on the caribou trail, where he had gone his way;
As he turned in his track and doubled back across a dozen streams,
And hidden saw how the men of the law, were caught in his cunning
    schemes.
But the snows grew deep and hunger's creep had thinned him to a ghost,
And each day showed the "Mountie Code," was not an idle boast.
And now the might of his six-foot height, was but an empty shell,
He fought the blows of the driven snows, and a thousand times he fell.

O'er storming waste he ploughed in haste, though his feet were things of
    lead,
And forward and back they followed his track, as over the wilds he fled;
O'er crag and hill with iron will, he dragged his frozen form,
And over the creeks and the Yukon peaks, the blizzard hurled its storm.
And the ice-winds pierced, and the storms were fierce and unrelenting
    foes,
In the dingy grey of feeble day, he stumbled in the snows;
And ever the law came down the draw that was the river bed,
With bushmen's skill they hugged each hill, remembering their dead.

The trapper turned while bullets burned, and blasted in the snow,
And, deadly aimed, his rifle flamed, and laid a Mountie low.
A leaden hail swept o'er the trail, and smashed the trapper down,
Behind his pack in the battle wrack, he fired at the men of the Crown;
And round the draw crept the men of the law, with rifles sighted low,
And a hail of lead to the trapper sped, and his body slumped in the snow;
And he didn't rise with red-rimmed eyes, and leap and shoot and slay,
As he had done with flaming gun, upon that other day.

For Death had crushed queer thoughts that rushed and tumbled in his
    mind,
And bitter cold and hunger's hold, all that was left behind;
And his blackened hands were icy bands, stiff as his frozen legs,
And they showed how he'd lain at the well of pain, and drank it to the dregs.
This was the man whose hard trails ran from that grim Rat River fort,
Who hurled his flaws into broken laws, and found his fate was short.
On the "mystery roll" of the manhunt scroll, is written the trapper's name,
But no one knows just who he was, from whence or why he came.

Snowblind

—Superintendent C.E. Rivett-Carnac

Snow blindness often struck the members of a dog-sled patrol if the pupils of their eyes were not protected: the eyes would painfully close due to the fierce glare of the sun off the snow or sea ice. After a few days' rest, the eyes would improve, but sometimes there would be retina damage. C.E. Rivett-Carnac became the tenth commissioner of the Force in 1959. He was a true northerner and published a book titled Pursuit in the Wilderness *(Boston, Massachusetts, Little, Brown & Co., 1965). From* RCMP Quarterly, *1946.*

Almost out of sight we saw him, leaden-footed in the ice,
Just a tiny fly, slow-moving, on a tablecloth of white,
Staggering, falling, rising, calling, trapped within the Arctic vise,
With frozen sun above him, blinding in its spear-tipped light.

Fate had crept upon him quietly through the timeless winter days,
All unseen the ghosts had dogged him, talon-fingered, crooked to seize,
Day by day they'd followed after, watched the sun's expanding rays,
Rising slowly through the seasons from the far antipodes.

Now the Arctic sun had awakened, taken aim, and sped its dart,
Archer of the frozen heavens, aiming from the distant skies,
To the empty land below him with an easy practiced art,
Such the skill and such the judgment, aiming only for the eyes!

Thus the Archer of the Sun had found him, rainbow-coloured to disarm,
Lit the lonely trail before him with his golden-curtained lamp;
Day by day he'd marked it northward, heedless, thoughtless of alarm,
Thinking it his guiding beacon as he made his nightly camp.

Round and round the space-hung heavens moved the Archer on his quest,
Hungry-eyed for something moving on the snow-plain far below,
Never resting, never sleeping, in the east or in the west,
Circumambient, ever watchful, scanning all the ice plateau!

Many months had gone before him since he passed below the rim,
Left the jeweled world a-glitter in the silver of the moon;
Taking shafts and bow and quiver, climbing down the crimson brim
Of the frost-draped Arctic Ocean where it forms its vast lagoon.

Now again he'd come a-hunting as the Spring was given birth,
And the winter night departed on her velvet-cushioned feet;
And he lay, not quite in hiding, past the limits of the earth
With the dawn mist wrapped about him like a blossom-painted sheet.

Soon he peered above the world-lip, catching at his fiery bowstring,
Raised his shoulders gently ... gently ... as a hunter stalks his prey,
Fitted arrow to his longbow, sailing on a lifted gold wing ...
Raider of the northern heavens, now embarked on his foray!

Day by day he'd waited patient as each season ran its course,
Watching, wheeling, climbing higher where the ice-land stretched
        beneath,
Searching out each hiding shadow, daily gaining strength and force,
Till he saw the mortal moving, shuffle-footed, underneath!

Now the time had come for action! Now the Archer flexed his bow—
Kneeled, and aimed, and drew the bow-string ... drew it flaming to the
        chin;
Loosed—and watched the arrow set the nether-world aglow
As it sped toward its target ... and blinding entered in!

He was dead when we came near him, lying starkly on his back,
And his tortured eyes stared bloodshot at the skies cold biting light;
But the tale of what happened lay, in script, upon his track ...
Where he'd staggered, blind, in circles, when the sun blacked out his
        sight!

Voyage of Discovery

—W.O. Gidman, Ottawa, Ontario

Written and presented in 1958 to my future wife, Miss Claire Brunet, by a dear friend and colleague of hers at the Department of Northern Affairs and Natural Resources in Ottawa, Ontario. I had met Claire on the Canadian icebreaker C.D. Howe in Resolute Bay, Northwest Territories, in August 1958. Her friend understood our difficulties of distance and loneliness.

> In the deep dark breathless hush of a summer night
> When the world's asleep, though streets are light,
> And traffic's roar has given o'er,
> To the silent stars so bright;
> Thoughts of mine go winging, memories bringing,
> To someone alone, in a Mountie's home,
> To an island near the Pole.
> And then, of course, I wonder,
> As naturally would be,
> Does he too, in the darkness, ponder,
> And ever think of me?
>
> Recall he may the ship's old clanging bell,
> Measuring our hours together, too quickly and well,
> While the crashing ice like a giant's dice,
> Heaved upward on the swell.
> So strange to meet on an iron ship, winds sharp whip,
> At dazzling noon or soft polar moon,
> North of latitude seventy-three.
> Yet that became the loveliest trip,
> A girl could ever make;
> And perfect too; except that you,
> Have caused my heart to ache!
>
> Charming, delightful, it was thrilling to stand
> While the bow rose and fell, as we gazed at the land,
> Or I glimpsed in your eyes, sweet love's surprise,
> Or felt the warmth of your hand.
> I remember well our parting, tears were nearly starting,

As we turned there in the bay and the vessel moved away;
But when a bluff shut off the view
Then it seemed I quickly knew,
That more than just a friend I'd left behind,
And I also knew that I'd wait for you
And the love dear, that I left behind.

Two thousand miles a love to find,
A lonely girl, a long patrol,
And the water and snow and ice
A happy journey, a handsome Mountie,
Straight and strong, now a song,
Across the miles, happy smiles, and love.

RECRUITS, TRAINING, AND HORSES

Recruit's Dream Before and After

—Constable Forbes M. Murray, #11895

Since the establishment in 1883 of Depot Division, the training academy at Regina, many recruits have come and gone, each no doubt with bittersweet memories that lasted a lifetime. Training has been modernized, of course, but it was always strict and harsh, even more so in the days of the horses. Murray wrote approximately 80 poems during his early service in the 1930s, many of them referring to life in the Force in an era when the "mounted" aspect of a Mountie's life was the norm, and the care and maintenance of its horses were paramount (no pun intended). This poem was written circa 1933. From Wake the Prairie Echoes.

'Twas in the midst of summer
Beneath a bright blue sky
A young man one day was watching
A Mountie ride slowly by.
As he saw the man of the red coat
Who looked neither to right nor to left
And saw his prancing charger
And the man's broad powerful chest
With the sun on the red coat shining
Fair maidens looked on askance
Hoping for a smile from the Mountie
If he looked their way by chance.

The youth that watched the red coat
Thought how he would join the force
And saw himself in bright red serge
Seated on a prancing horse.
He pictured himself with a prisoner
To take to the county jail
At the point of a shiny revolver
For a Mountie could never fail.
He thought of how the girls would follow
If he gave them even a glance
And pictured himself as famous
In a life of great romance.

He thought how he'd capture wild Indians
In a land by the setting sun
How he'd roll up in his blanket
When the toil of day was done.
He would travel the great Mackenzie
And see the ice floes run
The Esquimaux in the Arctic
In the land of the midnight sun.
He would write back home to mother
And the sweetheart far behind
He would tell of his wild adventures
Fond fancies of his mind.
So dreamed the would-be Mountie
He resolved right there and then
That he would apply at the office
And be a "man among men."

Now we see the Mountie
A recruit as fresh and green
As cabbage in the nearby garden
But he has realized his dream.
For he is one of the Mounted
In a western training school
Being damned by hard-boiled corporals
For every kind of a fool.
He crawls out of bed in the morning
At early break of day,
To groom and clean the horses
And feed the oats and hay.

Instead of bands of Indians
In a land of great romance
He is polishing brass and buttons
And brushing the dust off his pants.
Or pushing a damned old shovel
And brushing the stable floor
Instead of chasing prisoners
With his six-gun's thundering roar.

If mother could only see him
Just pitching horse manure
Or that darling little sweetheart
It would break her heart for sure.
For instead of a brilliant red coat
To wear from morn 'till night
He is wearing a pair of stable pants
But his smile still is bright.
They may make him wash the dishes
Or scrub the mess room floor
But they can't stop him from dreaming
Of those dear old days of yore.

He is working for "King and Country"
For the force of the RCMP
It will take more than one day
Of oats and hay
To make of him a real Mountie.
The coat was not made for attraction
To catch the femmes' fond smiles
It stands for fear both far and near
And for Right o'er many a mile.
So it is that the dreams of the rookie
Are realized by the sweat of his brow
His red coat looks keen wherever he is seen
And he rides a charger now.
To dream of daring bandits
With their gold in a glittering pile
How on horseback he'd pursue them
For many a weary mile.

We Are Seven

—Constable Forbes M. Murray, #11895

Another paean by Constable Murray to the joys of horse tending. Written in 1933, when the author was in training, or perhaps on the RCMP Musical Ride. From Wake the Prairie Echoes.

Just seven went out to stables
At the close of a weary day
To bed down the Mountie horses
And feed the oats and hay.

We toiled, we worked, we sweated
With brush and shovel and broom
As if there wasn't another hour
Before the day of doom.

"Water those gol-durned horses,"
A voice was heard to say;
"A bale of straw, a tin of feed
Where in hell is all that hay?"

"Get over you long-faced critters;
Keep off my blooming feet."
Watering those forty horses
Isn't what you'd call a treat.

Bedding, watering, and feeding
Seven men where twenty should be;
A kick from a horse, a stab from a fork
It's all the same to me.

Brushes in a row, go down the room
Seven men and the thin brown line,
Chaff and dust rise up before
Like waves on the salty brine.

A rumble like distant thunder
Comes down the stable floor
'Tis but the old wheelbarrow
Coming through the feed-room door

Not only are the horses contented
As they munch the oats and hay,
The hungry men are now lined up
It's the close of a Mountie day.

The Educated Mountie

—Constable A.C. Nixon, #9746

The aspirations and ideals of a recruit prior to joining the Force. To "grab a collar" means to make an arrest. From RCMP Quarterly, *1936.*

I'll study Biology, also Psychology, Botany, Syntax and Germs,
I'll brush up on Cato, Confucius and Plato, and converse in classical
   terms.

I'll soak up Geology, also Pathology, no one's more willing than I,
I'll learn Infant Feeding, and follow Good Breeding, and Science Domestic
   I'll try.

I'll be Academic, Precise and Abstemic, of Knockabout Brawling and
   Strife,
And bear to my Station a Cosmic Relation, with a broad teeming
   Knowledge of Life.

Instead of the Fistic, I'll study the Mystic, Hypnotic Mesmeric I'll be.
When I grab a collar, 'twill be as a Scholar, and not as Low-Brow, you see.

In Science and Letters, I'll be of the Betters, and then, as a matter of
   course,
I'll gargle some Borax, and spray well my Thorax, and go get a job on the
   Force!

Musings of a Stable Orderly

—Constable Forbes M. Murray, #11895

Touching on his favourite subject again, Murray was inspired to write this poem after a regular officers' inspection at Depot Division.

Oh, that touch of sweetest fragrance
That comes to me today
While I clean those blooming stables
And feed the oats and hay.
It is wafted on the breezes
That smell so fine and pure
They always know I'm coming
It's the smell of horse manure.

If I ever hold commission
In the service of the king
I'll not forget the stables
Or one single little thing.
The corn broom, brush, and shovel
That stood behind the door
And all that damned old sawdust
We sprinkled on the floor.

For it seemed 'twas everlasting
That running back and fore
With the big broom and the shovel
Between the horses and the door.
If plugs were just invented
It would help the orderly
Who forever cleans the stables
For inspection Saturday.

In heaven, I often wonder,
If horses make a mess
If the angels clean the stables
I don't need second guess.
For they wouldn't be the angels

They were when they began
If they cleaned those blooming stables
Like our Mountie Stable Man.

The Recruit

—Corporal B.G. Boutilier, #14670

Written circa 1950. From Wake the Prairie Echoes.

This is the story they tell us
And here is the reason it's true
That there isn't a Force the world over
Like the Scarlet, the Gold, and the Blue.

I'm in the ranks of the recruits
We are still a bit clumsy and green.
In the words of the Sergeant who drills us:
"The WORST that I ever have seen!"

He told me I needed a haircut.
I said, "But I got one today!"
He yelled in my face, "Get another!"
Back talk to that Sergeant won't pay!

So I hied me away to the barber
And he trimmed it close down to the roots.
So then I got three days of Night Guard
Because I had dirt on my boots.

But then I can count myself lucky,
My punishment just doesn't rate
With the lad who got two weeks of duty
For parading just one minute late.

You've got to keep everything polished
And spotlessly neat in your room.
The unfortunate laddie who doesn't
Is good for a week with a broom.

The O.C. has weekly inspection
And let the recruits beware:
On a service revolver or rifle
He can see dust that's not even there!

Then yesterday on the parade square
I turned left, when ordered "Right turn!"
But I'll find left from right on the Night Guard;
I've been given a week more to learn.

But it's fun when they take us for swimming
Then next we're to shoot on the range
So it's back to the breeks, boots and Stetson,
With all of five minutes to change.

We take lots of "Physical Torture"
And often go out for a run.
The Corporal in charge says a mile,
I'll bet you it's five if it's one.

"Let's see you do 25 push-ups
Come on! Are you babies or men?"
Till we're heartsick, bone-tired and weary;
Then we do it all over again.

And then there's the stables and horses,
In such comfort and luxury they dwell!
And we'd all like the riding instructor
If he used us a quarter as well.

You're bound to get one that is skittish
(If you've never been on one before)
And I pity the one I've been riding
If his poor back is just half as sore.

There's some of the lads just can't take it.
They've been granted their discharge and quit.
But I think I'll be one to stay with it
Though I might get discouraged a bit.

For I've got a hunch that they're trying
To see just how much we can take
So I've made up my mind that I'll show them
I've the kind of heart they can't break.

And when I get through with my training
I'll be one with that legion of old,
And I'll take my proud place with the members
Of the Scarlet, the Blue, and the Gold.

So You'd Like to Be a Mountie

—Anonymous

A Mountie's life was nothing if not regimented. Written circa 1952, from Wake the Prairie Echoes.

So you'd like to be a Mountie, wearing a Stetson hat,
Scarlet tunic, Breeks, High boots, Revolver, and things like that.
Riding around on a nice big horse, carrying carbine and lance;
Well here's some of the things you have to do before you get that chance.

Up at the sound of Reveille, up with a grin and a jump,
Stretching the kinks out of your back (where your mattress has a hump)
Down to the gym for P.T., then "Stables," the trumpeter calls,
And away you go to groom your horse after cleaning out the stalls.

Horse to be fed and watered, saddle and bridle to clean,
Polish and shine your equipment till you're sure it's fit to be seen;
Shave and wash up for breakfast, off to the mess room you go,
When the trumpeter sounds "Cook-house," you find it don't pay to be slow.

Get dressed and "Fall In" for "Inspection." Tho' you're sure you'd dazzle the eye,
You feel your insides tremble, till the O.C. passes by;
Then you glimpse the Sergeant-Major strut with his chest stuck out,
And you know the Inspection passed O.K. Boy, you could almost shout.

"Boots and Saddles" for Practice Ride; Walk, March, Canter and Trot;
Around in a circle, then Figure Eight, till you're covered with dust, and hot;
Stop then to "Breathe" the horses, and maybe adjust your gear,
And longingly glance at the shade of a tree where you'd like to pound your ear.

Back to the stables at noon-time, "Unsaddle and Feed" hay and grain.
You wonder what's on for the p.m., as you head for the mess room again;
You're hoping that it'll be lectures (to give you a chance to rest)
It's going to take some study to pass that final test.

You find when you've had your dinner that it's lecture for an hour,
Then you're out for "Foot and Arms" drill, and does that turn you sour;
You're sure to get tangled up a bit and forget your "Left and Right,"
But you're bally sure of one thing—you're going to sleep at night.

Back to stables for "Evening Feed," then off to supper you go;
You casually glance at the "Order Board" and find to your deepest woe,
You are up for "Night Guard" and "Picquet," and under your breath mumble,
    "Well—
It's nice to be dressed up for duty, but this training sure is—?????"

The Sergeant-Major's Prayer

—Corporal W.G. Kerr, #7685

Almost all recruits in training feared or respected the sergeants-major, who were almost always controlling, efficient to more than a fault, and even considered heartless. Written in the 1930s. From RCMP Quarterly *and* Wake the Prairie Echoes.

Lord of the realm of Limbo,
God of all soulless men,
Set me free from your bondage;
And make me human again.

Soften my raucous bellow,
That sets me as one apart;
Return the least of my virtues
Please give me back a heart.

Let me look at my fellows
And see them as flesh and blood;
Not as brands from the burning,
To be quenched by a vocal flood.

Free me from seeing damnation
In a visible spot of dust;
A dull unshining button
Or the faintest sign of rust.

Let not a grimy boot heel
Act as a gauge of worth;
Or a crease in an issue blanket
Be the foulest crime on earth.

Blind me to scanning pass-lists
When the clock is half past ten;
To know of those who find surcease
In taking the pleasures of men.

Give me a sense of values
To see as a place of doom,
And not as a seat of virtue,
The Division orderly room.

Make me the Sergeant-Major
That I prayed a man could be
When someone else was "Herod"
And the guy in the ranks was me.

S/M Absolute

—Dr. Will R. Bird

Written circa 1940, another tribute to the recruit's favourite character.

Beneath the breezy banner tree
The Sergeant-Major stands;
The chief a mighty man he is,
With well-remembered hands.
And the bawling of his minstrelsy
Is loud as brazen bands.

Day in, day out, from morn till night,
You may hear his bellows blow;
Confounding non-coms, in their plight,
Who know not where to go;
Till finally they take their flight,
Where canteen comforts flow.

Let full parade in order come,
And every mount be picked.
'Tis then that many a bobbing bum
By caustic wit is licked;
The Grand Panjandrum makes things hum,
In language none too strict.

Back on the left, dress up the right,
Confound your spurs and hocks;
Was ever circus such a sight
Since monkeys lost their blocks?
Then panic, by its sordid blight,
The whole procession locks.

Boiling, rejoicing, borrowing,
Onward through life he goes;
And now? 'Tis said, though sorrowing,
He met one on the nose;
But, in the regimental ring,
He flattened out his foes.

Thanks, from all ranks, my lordly friend,
For the lessons thou hast taught;
Thus at the forge of life we bend
Each wayward deed and thought,
Till Sergeant-Majors have an end,
Where they get all they ought.

Camp Wascana

—Sergeant B.G. Meyrick, #4479

Written during the 1920s and patterned on Longfellow's "Hiawatha." Situated near Wascana Creek, the original NWMP post of the same name became the NWMP headquarters in 1882. In 1885, the name changed to Depot Division and is in present-day Regina. The area was once known as "Pile of Bones," a reference to buffalo bones lying along the creek. From RCMP Quarterly *and* Wake the Prairie Echoes.

> On the banks of the Wascana
> Lo, there stands a big encampment
> Which is known throughout the country
> As the Red Coats' training depot.
> It is not a place of comfort
> Or of ease or recreation,
> But a place to get away from
> As recruits do in the evening.
> In one corner stands the tepee
> Of the Big White Chief's assistant;
> In another is the wigwam
> Where the medicine-man comes daily,
> He who mixes mystic potions,
> He who says, "Just put your tongue out,"
> Ere he sends you back to duty.
> In a third unsheltered corner
> Is the place of many tombstones
> And of little concrete crosses;
> In this little spot sequestered
> Lie the bones of former warriors
> Who have passed beyond the sunset
> To the grounds of happy hunting.

In the one remaining corner
Stands a gaunt forbidding structure
Which was recently erected,
By a scrupulous contractor
At a cost of sixty thousand,
Goodly dollars of the treasury
In this "hall of fame" each morning,
Bits and buckles all a-sparkle,
May be seen a group of riders
Going through their evolutions,
At the gentle instigation
Of instructors whose deportment
Would convey a strong impression,
That their matutinal slumbers
Had been prematurely ended.
Though they be not great of stature
These instructors know their business.
And the doughty Sergeant-Major
Sees that others know it also
As he brandishes his blacksnake,
With a smile like clouds of thunder.

In this dreadful torture chamber
Long and oft the riders suffer
As they breathe unholy curses
'Pon the brigands who invented
Forms of torture such as riding
With crossed stirrups and arms folded.
Come with me and I will show you
From the safety of the gallery
Pulsing nostrils filled with tan-bark,
Sweating faces dust-beclouded
That you cannot recognize them,
While outside upon the rooftop
Shrills a meadow lark enraptured
With the joy of spring's warm sunshine.

But lest you be nauseated
With this scene of human suffering,
Let us see another aspect;
Let's perambulate the sports field.
Here we see more budding warriors
Who with robot-like precision
Execute amazing movements
While an apoplectic sergeant
Utters incoherent war whoops,
Unintelligible war whoops
Such as scandalize the ladies,
Where the Braves display their prowess
With their shooting-sticks a-glitter,
Muttering acrid imprecations
On what they describe as useless
Sabre-rattling, till the welkin
Rings with protest unrestrained;
And the corporals assisting
In the role of drill instructors
Add their quota to the tumult.

See the column marches hither,
Marches thither, turning, wheeling,
Jostling, pushing, doubling, walking,
Till they reach the wooden sidewalk
Slimy with its film of gumbo.
And as each man treads more firmly
Forth they sally to the precincts
Of administrative buildings,
And when just outside the windows
Of the chiefs who sit in conclave
And of those whose office duties
Call for utmost concentration,
Inexorably they're halted
To receive loud admonitions
On the step that they've been keeping,
On the way they swing their right arms
And when due time has been given
To create a good impression

And sufficient interruption
In affairs within the office,
On they journey to dismissal,
And in hectic fifteen minutes
To prepare them for a lecture.

As we wait for "Evening Stables,"
See that lithe and supple figure
With a trumpet 'neath his armpit;
See him amble to the flagpole,
Scarce a lad of sixteen summers,
As he grapples with the halyards
And the good flag comes fluttering
To the ground at sound of "Sunset."

Now the warriors are assembling
In their jail-like stable jackets
With their grooming kits beside them.
Near them stands the Sergeant-Major
With his erudite assistant,
He who says "You'll be for Night Guard,"
He who says "Why were you absent
From the Sick Parade this morning?"
And when all preliminaries
Such as Roll Call and Inspection
Are completed, when "All Present"
Is stentoriously reported
To the officer on duty,
With a swinging gait that wavers
Like the great Atlantic breakers,
Moves the party to the stables
To commune with long-faced comrades
With too obvious reluctance;
There to gather the aroma
Of wet straw and filthy bedding
Which is subsequently carried
On their garments to the mess room.
Such the stench, one cannot wonder
That when mixed with smell of foodstuffs

One becomes a thing abhorrent
Even to one's boon companions.

But there comes an end to all things,
E'en monotony and tedium
Have their limits; e'en the patience
Of an editor is finite;
And lest I should be indicted
On a charge of too much verbiage
Let me hasten to assure you
There are sundry other aspects
Which may well be relegated
To a subsequent edition.
Thus we leave the mental pictures
Of the Pile-O'-Bones encampment
As we steal away in silence
In the gathering of the shadows,
In the aftermath of sunset,
With the twittering of the night-birds,
And the requiem of nature.

Among My Souvenirs

—Assistant Commissioner T.B. Caulkin

This poem takes a humorous look at a Mountie's rise through the ranks. Assistant Commissioner Caulkin spent many years in the Arctic and had a long, varied career. Written in the 1940s, from RCMP Quarterly *and* Wake the Prairie Echoes.

I joined the jolly old Mounted,
As a Special I shovelled coal;
I wanted to join as a Regular,
That was my ultimate goal.

But I lacked in education,
Was told to study some more,
So I purchased a Code and some Statutes,
And buried myself in their lore.

I eventually passed my tests, Sir,
And was taken on as a Sub.
You see I was underage then,
Only a bit of a cub.

So when I reached my majority,
I was given the rank of Third Grade
And started to study the pros and cons
Of just how a charge is laid.

I swatted my Code and the Manual,
The Statutes and how to use gas;
I studied the New Regulations,
And eventually managed to pass.

I became a second-class Constable,
And got an increase in pay,
Bought me a tux and a pair of spats,
And put in a pass for a day.

Then having returned to my studies,
My exams were easy to pass;
And oh, how I threw out my chest, Sir,
When promoted to rank of First Class.

"Keep up the good work," said the Sergeant,
"You'll soon have the same rank as I,
If 'Duty' you take for your motto
Then your only limit's the sky."

The science we call fingerprinting
Left my poor brain a bit overcome
For the crookedest part of a crook is
His straight-looking finger or thumb.

The purchase of books was a worry,
I never was out of the red;
It certainly empties one's pockets
To fill in the top of his head.

I eventually went on Detachment,
And managed my first arrest.
I booked a chap on the Excise Act
And awaited results of the test.

'Twas a potent concoction called Homebrew
So a charge had to be preferred
You'll pardon my pride in the Courtroom,
As I heard all the details aired.

A shot, then the scream of a woman
As the cork of an exhibit popped.
Three months at H.L. was the sentence,
This brewing has got to be stopped.

I attended Instruction Classes
The time was considered ripe
My award for three months of study
Was a beautiful coveted stripe.

A full-blown Acting Lance Corporal
Was the term applied to me,
I felt like a ruddy old admiral
With responsibility.

And early every morning
I'd strut the barrack square;
I figured myself the answer
To any young maiden's prayer.

The goal of my life's ambition
Was the rank of Staff, With Pay,
But now I'm discharged to Pension,
Old Age blocked my way.

RCMP Dream Fulfilled

—Ms. Joyce M. Pasemko

*Recited by Ms. Pasemko at the graduation of her daughter, Constable Pamela
J. Wilson, #35812, from RCMP training in Regina in 1980. A mother's love and
pride are most evident in this tribute.*

When she wasn't much more than a cherubic four
She could steal your heart with ease,
Her impish grin hid many a sin
As she charmed the birds from the trees.

Then the formative years, slightly dampened with tears,
When the fledgling tries out her wings,
When all you can do is watch and wait
To see what tomorrow brings.

They were bittersweet years, growing up can be hard,
She walked in the rain and the sun,
But all of the mountains God gave to her climb,
She climbed them, one by one.

As the years drift by on the tides of time
And fade like a rainbow trail,
I weigh the good times against the bad
And by far, the good prevail.

Looking back, I'd not change her, I'm happy for her
As her dreams seem about to unfold,
And I see her stand tall with her eyes on the flag,
Proudly wearing the blue and the gold.

LIFE AND DUTY

RCMP

—Corporal A.M. Veitch, #9276

In this poem, written around 1940, the author describes the far-flung regional divisions of the Force with tongue in cheek. "Andy" Veitch celebrated his 100th birthday in October 1999. From Wake the Prairie Echoes.

We live in the land of the Maple
'Neath the flag of the Red, White and Blue,
We enforce good British Justice,
In a way that Britishers do.

We patrol from Atlantic Ocean,
West to the Pacific Coast,
We are taught to be fair, true and useful,
And "Maintiens le Droit" is our boast.

Our members patrol the Arctic,
And pal with ice, husky, and snow,
They live more or less like a "native,"
In the land of the brave Eskimo.

Our duties are ever-changing,
Keeping pace with Canadian life,
Such changes are for a good reason,
The soothing of all public strife.

We are Policeman, Doctor and Bushman,
Soldier, Sailor and Nurse,
Stenographer, Bookkeeper, Lawyer,
And a few other things that are worse.

Our Force is divided in districts,
Or Divisions more properly known,
If you ask which of these is the best one,
Each member will claim it's his own.

There's "E" tucked away at Vancouver,
City of Rain, Sunshine and Hope,
Where they spend their time grooming horses,
And harassing the Chinese for "dope."

There's "B" 'neath the hill at old Dawson,
In the land of Furs, Timber and Cold,
Where Old Timers gather 'round box-stoves,
And famed Yukon yarns are retold.

There's "K" located at Edmonton,
On soil which the Indians found,
Where the Force built a good reputation,
Which is Honest, True, Faithful and Sound.

There's "G" now located at Ottawa,
In the shadow of Parliament Hill,
They're the boys who patrol the Arctic,
And thrive on the wintry chill.

There's "Depot" and "F" at Regina,
In the heart of the Canadian West,
"F" keeps a check on the "crimesters,"
At "Depot" it's drill at its best.

There's dirty old "D," as they termed it,
Now located at Winnipeg fair,
Near the famous Red River Valley,
That we hear of so much on the air.

There's "A" and "Headquarters" at Bytown,
The former are guarding our Gold,
The latter compile all instructions,
And insure that we do as we're told.

"C" by the mighty St. Lawrence,
In Montreal, fair City of Beer,
Where alcohol entered in car loads,
Is transformed into bottles of cheer.

"H" is found down at Halifax,
The City of Salt, Fish and Boats.
Where the Force has a good reputation,
For getting the 'Rum Runners' Goats."

Then "J" operates in New Brunswick,
From the City of Fredericton bright,
Where they claim to be hard-working fellows,
And are busy from morning till night.

There's "N" by the river at Rockcliffe,
In the wide open spaces they smirk,
Where they raise husky dogs for the Arctic,
Apart from their regular work.

"L" is located at Charlottetown,
On the Isle of Potatoes and God,
Where they get many clues from the natives,
By keeping their ears to the Sod.

Then there's "O"—excuse me for breathing,
I'm not often given to jest,
It's located in dear Old Toronto,
And to me it's as good as the best.

Thus do the men of the "Mounted,"
Distribute their work with their play,
They toil, fight and freeze for their country,
Thus ensuring their pensions and pay.

The QM's Slogan

—Sergeant B.G. Meyrick, #4479

The Quartermaster Store handled all needs and field requirements, and tending it was a monotonous job. Written in the 1930s, from RCMP Quarterly, *1937.*

In eighteen hundred and seventy-four, a "Quarter-bloke" toiled in the
  Q.M. Store;
His ledger was neat and his helpers good, he hadn't much pay but plenty
  of food.
With surplus stores from mysterious source, no shortage should ever
  occur, of course;
But despite the greatest possible care, discrepancies crept in here and
  there.

"I'll teach these beggars," at length said he, "to wish discrepancies on to
  me."
And thereupon he evolved a plan to cope with errors; and he began
  requiring recipients
Everywhere to acknowledge receipt with the utmost care; so in covering
  letters
A "sine qua non" was: "PLEASE ACKNOWLEDGE RECEIPT HEREON."

In the interim many have come and gone, robust and ruddy or pale and
  wan,
One-foot-in-the-grave, or cadaverous cough, with stores "expended" or
  "struck off."
Soul-killing monotony still holds sway, the same as it did in that bygone
  day; and the
Quarter-bloke's slogan lingers on: "PLEASE ACKNOWLEDGE RECEIPT
  HEREON."

The Orderly Room and Headquarters

—Constable Forbes M. Murray, #11895

In this poem, in contrast to his others in this collection, Murray seems to miss stable duties a bit, as he turns his critical eye to the even more mundane aspects of office work, which were the order of every day. Written in the 1930s, from Wake the Prairie Echoes.

No need for spurs and breeches, no need for belt and gun
No grooming in the mornings, no stables when we're done.

Such a life of wild adventure, we are Mounties, don't you see
Pounding a noisy typewriter, looking for the missing key.

Alas! There are no bandits, no riding the open plain
No Indians on the rampage, I have searched for them in vain.

We are the men of the Mounted, there are women working too,
The "silent force" is not silent, when there's typing work to do.

Then why that pained expression, on our handsome Sergeant's face?
Is it a type-o-graphical error? Did he forget to leave a space?

I am sure there isn't a bandit, hiding beneath his chair
Although he seems to be worried, and is searching everywhere.

Oh, such a life of romance, wild adventure, don't you see
Although we are in the office, Headquarters of the RCMP.

A Saga of the Mounted

—Anonymous

The monotony of wartime duties in Montreal were relieved somewhat by sorties to various nightclubs in the big city. Written circa 1940, from Scarlet and Gold, *1975.*

Of strange things I sing
'Neath the Sun Life Building:
Of the men of Scarlet and Gold,
Of policeman Jollee,
And old Slug Magee
And Constable Archer so bold.

Through the long hours of the night
They watch and they fight
To keep wide awake and alert
For they are out gunning
For saboteurs cunning,
On that you can bet your last shirt.

Though far from the sunshine,
They'll not grumble nor whine,
But their duty they'll do with a smile
While the air's a bit crappy
And they are tired and slaphappy,
They're right on the job all the while.

As Officer Bellig strides to and fro'
He dreams of his home in the West:
When this bloody war's over
He'll be back in the clover
And sagebrush and dust he knows best.

We've been to the Brewery,
And Hotel de Ville,
We've been to the Tick-Tock as well.
Tomorrow we go to the Club Val d'Or,
And from there we go straight to bed.

I've amused myself while writing this verse,
So my pencil, I'm willing to lend it,
If anyone thinks he can do better or worse,
'Cause I'm darned if I know how to end it.

The Aftermath

—Constable J.J. Parker

Back to work at RCMP headquarters in Ottawa. The workaday world seems less than inspiring, especially after a vacation—a feeling many workers have no doubt experienced. Written in the 1930s, from Wake the Prairie Echoes.

Vacation days are over, and we're back to the same old grind.
Back to the same old chair and desk (with the work three weeks behind)
Back to the same old signing the same old book in the hall,
Back to the same old office with the same old marks on the wall.

Back to the same old waiting on the corner for the same old car,
Where the same old lad is smoking the same old chewed-up cigar,
Back to the same old troubles, the same old headaches and ills,
To the same old worrying how and when to pay the same old bills.

Back to the same—but say now, just in case we forget—
There'll be no ants in the sugar at the table tonight—you bet,
No wasps around the jam-jar, no sand or grit in the food,
And we'll sleep tonight on a mattress, boy—ain't that something good?

Yes, vacation days are over, but somehow we seem to find
That we're back to the same old routine with a fresher, clearer mind,
Facing our cares and duties with much less worry and fear,
And plan—in our idle moments—for vacation again, next year.

Midnight Patrol

—Constable Lionel W. Broadway, #11772

Written circa 1934, this poem describes enforcement action by two Mounties on night patrol near Edmonton, Alberta.

When all is still and silence reigns
And darkness covers roads and lanes
There ventures forth from out its hole
The Mounted Police Midnight Patrol.

Two constables on duty bent
Went forth one night with full intent
To search the highways and the low
To fill all evil ones with woe.

Beeching drove the speedy hack
For on this night a date had Jack
And partnered by the worthy Jones
He took the wheel with stifled groans.

So, 'neath the light of twinkling stars
They hunted for suspicious cars
They checked up lights both front and rear
And watched for liquor, wine and beer.

Although they wandered here and there
Offenders seemed most scarce and rare
But suddenly from out the night
A shapeless object loomed in sight.

Buck Jones stared, then HALT! he cried
Beeching at once the brakes applied
For parked beside the road they saw
A car suspicious to the law.

Through open door our Buck then spied
Two lovers seated side by side
And 'twixt the two he further saw
A crock of wine upon the floor.

The man consuming in this way
Had five-and-twenty dollars to pay
So, "would-be parkers" are forewarned
The Police Patrol must not be scorned.

When Beeching, Lionel, Jones and Jake
Or others are out upon the "beat"
They take full notice of the facts
Enforcing all Provincial Acts.

The Graveyard Shift

—Ms. Lela McKay

The other side of the midnight shift as seen by a policeman's wife. This poem reveals the constraints imposed on a policeman's family life, and his wife's fears and tribulations about the dangerous nature of his job. From RCMP Quarterly *and* Wake the Prairie Echoes.

So it's the graveyard shift you call it,
That dreary midnight round to dawn;
But there are other names to fit
Those dragging hours that you are gone.

Am I a coward to lie in bed
And fear the house afire, or see
The hosts of terrors yet unread,
Unleashed, and very real to me?

Yet with the day and you, my dear,
My phantoms of the night dispelled
I laugh with same, at foolish fear
My lonely mind alone impelled.

But you must sleep, so through the day
The baby must not laugh or cry;
Nor throw her blocks or pail in play
Though she's too young to tell her why.

The piano played by neighbour's child,
The builder's hammer, saw and blast,
Nerves on edge and temper riled
When you, still tired, arise at last.

It's hell for you, the graveyard shift,
But worse for me, I will contend.
You get a daily few hours' lift,
But I rest not 'til its long-drawn end.

The Mountie's Wife

—Anonymous

Dave Brisbin, a retired RCMP member from Tecumseh, Ontario, observes: "She was required to be versatile, capable and flexible to suit her husband's career." Dave received this poem in 1996 from an elderly friend, who said the friend who'd given it to her had told her the author was unknown. Written in the 1940s.

Who said, "Variety is the spice of life?"
No doubt it was first said by a Mountie's wife:
For the poor girl never knows just where she's at,
Her home is wherever he parks his hat.
She moves every two years into new sets of quarters,
During which time she raises sons or daughters.
She packs up to move to "K" or "A"
Then orders are changed and they go to "J."
Her home may be a hut with no room for expansion
It may be a trailer, or perhaps a Governor's Mansion
Then she uncrates the furniture in rain or snow
While her husband is off with the NCO.

She no more than gets settled when she must dress up pretty
And go to a party and be charming and witty.
She must know contract rules, mah jong and chess,
And whether a straight or a flush is best.
On every subject she must know how to discourse
She must curl, ski, and golf, and perhaps ride a horse.
She jitterbugs with constables who are always glamorous
And waltzes with officers who are usually amorous.
She must drink all concoctions, gin, whiskey, and beer
But, of course, moderately, or she'll wreck his career.

He insists on economy, questions every cheque stub,
Yet her house must be run like a hotel or club.
For she entertains at all hours, both early and late
For any number of guests, eighty or eight.
On the first and fifteenth of each month there is plenty of cash
So she serves steaks and chicken, but the last week, it's hash.
That there will be a bank balance she has no assurance,
It all goes for likker, or some darned insurance.

At an age to retire he is still hale and hearty,
Fit as a fiddle, and the life of the party.
While she is exhausted, and a little nervous,
Really a wreck after his thirty-five years' service.
But even then, when all is said and done,
She still believes a Mountie's life is fun.
She has loved every minute, and why—good grief,
She'd have been bored with a doctor or merchant chief.
But there's one free issue that all Mounties wear,
It's the long-service medal that she should share.

Government Oats

—Constable Cecil E. Morgan, #1749

A policeman dishonest! Possibly a bit of fact here. Written in 1934.

I will tell you a story, I tell it with grief,
Because, all unwittingly, I was a thief.
I was young—inexperienced—and thought it a sin
To steal a tomato, or even a pin.
Yet I'm bound to confess in these personal notes
That I once stole a bushel of Government oats.

It was out at High River, when driving a team—
Of stealing one oat grain I never would dream—
That I drove forty miles in to Shorty McGee's,
Where they gave me three dollars to put up my gees.
When nearing November they cut off the grant,
"What, sleep in the open—you certainly shan't,"
Said Shorty: "Just drop off a sack of oats here,
And both you and your horses shall have the best cheer."

To this devilish whisper I paid foolish heed
And dumped off those oats. Oh, the terrible deed,
But Nemesis caught me—as surely will he,
All those who steal oats. He and Staff Sergeant B.,
Who counted the sacks, and remarked properly,
"On the peg, my fine lad, stealing Government property."
I could hardly believe it, but saw in his face
No chance to escape from this awful disgrace
And I knew it was hopeless to beg him to save
My mother's grey hairs from a sorrowful grave.

The boys, who all liked me, and not Sergeant B.,
Were sorrowful too at the fate of poor me.
There was much thinking done, and much plotting to save
My poor mother's hairs from a sorrowful grave.

The time it was nearing when, gyves upon wrists,
I to Calgary go, Sergeant B. still insists,
When sitting with Freke, who was smarter than I,
Two whacking great pigs caught that Constable's eye.
"Eureka! I've found it," he cried with an oath,
"Those pigs are B.'s porkers and I brought them both
In my wallets from Stinson's—and look at them now:
They're two hundred a piece—Why, boy, it's a wow!
If you'd stolen ten bushels, you'd win in a walk,
For B. has four hundred of good oat-fed pork.
It's a fact. The Detachment can swear, to a man,
That his pigs have been oat-fed—deny it who can."
So B. reconsidered and thought it was best
To forget that he ever put me in arrest.

That Little Red-Bound Manual

—Constable Forbes M. Murray, #11895

That little but mighty red manual had to be studied and followed. Written in 1934. From RCMP Quarterly *and* Wake the Prairie Echoes, *1973.*

That little red-bound manual
Every Mountie knows it well
If only it had the gift of speech
What stories it could tell
Of those that long have gone before
From out this mighty force
Who read its well-worn pages
For better or for worse.

In our law that little manual
Has always had a hand
Though it's not among the law books
Or on our greatest judges' stand.
Each Mountie knows its value
They have learned the lesson well.
On everyone within this force
It has cast its magic spell.

We read within the pages
Of the great "Esprit de Corps"
Which holds the force together
In peacetime or in war.
It tells of all the pathways
We must and must not tread
It's writ with the blood of heroes
Whose fame will ever spread.

That little red-bound manual
Is not a book of verse,
It will help the studious reader,
And make the lazy curse.
No Shakespeare, Burns, or Shelley

Have penned those lines to read,
Though they're full of inspiration
For everyone in need.

If you want detective stories
That will thrill you through and through
Just read that little manual,
That is all you have to do.
But remember great detectives
Are never found in print,
They are made by patient study,
Their work they never stint.

Within that little manual
Fiction holds a place
Just read what's writ between the lines,
Great stories you will trace
Of heroes in the Yukon,
And the Arctic's frozen space
From Atlantic to Pacific
You will find our mighty race.

That little red-bound manual
Is in our training school
And is often used as a weapon
For the head of a passing fool.
Always treat your manual
As a true and trusty friend
Never use it harshly,
It will pay you in the end.

That little red-bound manual
Has a long and trusted arm
That connects up every city
With every little farm.
Its agents are the Mounted
In East, West, South, and North
Who read this Mountie gospel
Before they travel forth.

That little red-bound manual
So tattered, marked, and torn
Despise it not as useless
Or treat it as forlorn.
It holds a place to envy
In this great and mighty land
It has often walked with danger
On each and every hand.

That little red-bound manual
May fade in years to come
But there is satisfaction
In duty that's well done.
Learn a lesson from your manual
And read its pages well
Not once will it betray you
Untruths it will never tell.

It should rank among the famous
In books that hold a place
Among the greatest authors
It could hold a shining face.
Fame is not its virtue
It is like our mighty force
Pursuing duty silently
For better or for worse.

Maintiens le Droit

—Constable F.J. Smith, #8470

"Maintain the Right" is the proud motto of the Force. From Scarlet and Gold *and* Wake the Prairie Echoes.

A Guidon waves with its battle song
A message of service brave and long
From a famous Force with its deeds untold
Proud of its colours, Scarlet and Gold.

With the Scarlet and Gold is the colour of Blue,
Denoting a service which comes anew
In Arctic seas and storm-tossed waves
To "maintiens le droit" this service braves.

A haven of refuge have they none
'Till the voyage is finished and duty done
Nothing romantic in Marine man's toil
To "maintiens le droit" and villains foil.

In cloud-flecked skies the Air Patrol
Speed with the wind to a destined goal
To "maintiens le droit" or duty render
With orders to aid and service tender.

Men, planes, ships, dogs, and horses,
All are used in combined forces
From lowly rank to high degree
Justice is served with loyalty.

ROYAL, an honour great upon them vested
CANADIAN, justice is fairly tested
MOUNTED, on crest and standard to read
POLICE, "maintiens le droit" their founders' creed.

With solemn sound and stately tread
A requiem hovers for the dead,
With duty done they nobly served,
From "maintiens le droit" they never swerved.

RCMP First Canadian Division

—Private W. Grieve

The diverse duties of members of the Force included those of provost, or military police, during the Second World War. Major L..H. Nicholson, MBE, was the overall commander of the provost, and in 1951 he became the ninth commissioner of the Force. Written in the 1940s, from Wake the Prairie Echoes.

They keep the lifelines open as far as you can go,
On the frontal arteries, control the ebb and flow,
As a gun is to the layer, as a ship is to the crew,
The roads are to the Mounties, with credit overdue.

Everything seems all serene, as the convoy rolls along,
The engines purring softly while we hum a little song,
At the bridges and diversions, standing guard for you,
There will be a Provost man to stop, or see you through.

When things are topsy-turvy, just reason out the fault,
Speeding, nine times out of ten, brought you to a halt,
Please respect the Provost signs, on view along the road,
You have responsibilities, and they also have a load.

Perhaps you've made St. Vito, on a leave of forty-eight
Sampled some old vino and begun to feel your weight,
Keep away from "Out of Bounds," do not start up rough,
A "Seventy-Nine" may appear and surely call your bluff.

Or in Divisional area you may have lost the way,
Try to contact one of them, and everything's Okay,
We all "slip up" sometime, go Left instead of Right,
Even in a bawling-out, they will treat you white.

Way back home in Canada, they always got their man,
Compliments in Italy are "situation's well in hand,"
In the Div. they form a link, shellfire cannot sever,
Monty says, "We'll see it through, you and I together."

Their Majesties

—Superintendent T.B. Caulkin

Written following the royal visit of King George VI and Queen Elizabeth to Canada in 1939, just before the war. From RCMP Quarterly, *circa 1940.*

God bless you, King of Canada, and Queen Elizabeth too,
Your visits to our homeland, are honestly too few.
You came and saw and conquered, a gracious pair we met
We tried to pay our homage, in a way you won't forget.

We waved our flags and shouted, hip-hip and hip-hoo-ray,
And despite the threatening weather, we all turned out to stay.
We lined the routes in thousands, and took our lunches too,
We meant to see your Majesties, as you were passing through.

And as your cortege came along, our cheers were loud and true.
The tears coursed down our glowing cheeks, we thought so much of you.
From Atlantic to Pacific, you made your stately way.
You won the hearts of everyone, "Will ye no come back to stay."

To the roll of drums and bugle call, the peal of bells in towers tall,
And the boom of guns in yonder wood, were omens grand of all that's
        good.
You performed your scheduled duties, in an ever-gracious way,
And indulged in many sidelines, as you progressed through each day.

You took time out for veterans, the sick, the aged and poor,
The tears welled up into our eyes, as we saw you more and more.
Her Majesty always with a smile, just won our hearts, we loved her style.
As fair a lass as could be seen, we're proud to think that she's our Queen.
Here's health unto Your Majesties, God Bless Your Happy Reign,
Your visit's been a brilliant one, "Will you no come back again."

Marching Song

—J.C. Martin, K.C., Weyburn, Saskatchewan

A lawyer pays tribute to the Force. Written in the 1950s, from RCMP Quarterly *and* Wake the Prairie Echoes.

There was a day when hunters roamed the prairie vast and brown;
Then, gentlemen adventurers possessed it for the Crown,
Until the new-born Canada, a nation yet to be,
Made British North America extend from sea to sea.

When settlers came upon the plain to till their lonely farms,
And when rebellion reared its head with tumult and alarms,
When thousands crossed the Chilcoot Pass, led on by gold's allure,
The Mountie ever went ahead to make the way secure.

The Mountie is not mounted now, except on a machine,
His horse is all but mem'ry, in the age of gasoline;
He makes his vigilant patrols, in air, on land, and sea,
And helps to keep this Canada the freest of the free.

The tunic of the Mountie is far more than just a coat;
'Tis the symbol of his duty, of his word pledged to devote
His mind, his strength, his talents, and withal a courage keen
To maintain the rights and safety of the subjects of the Queen.

A Job for the Mounted

—Constable F.E. Torpey, #5314

The "Limited" is believed to have been a train. Constable Torpey served in the RNWMP for approximately four years. Written circa 1912, this poem is part of the Torpey Papers, a collection at the RCMP Museum, Regina, Saskatchewan. From Wake the Prairie Echoes, *1973*

> Only the Limited rushing along,
> Only a spark in the rye-grass long,
> Only the breath of a wind that's strong,
> Then—a job for the Mounted Police.
>
> Only some boys in a shack at night,
> Only a word and a flash that's bright,
> Only a cry to the silent night,
> Then—a job for the Mounted Police.
>
> Only a thrill at a story told
> Only a spirit less wise than bold,
> Only a bed in the snow so cold,
> Then—a job for the Mounted Police.
>
> Only a case of sickness here,
> Only a pain and a little fear,
> Only a case of "nobody near,"
> Then—a job for the Mounted Police.

The RCMP Band

—Anonymous

The first Mounted Police band was formed in July 1874, during the Great March West. It continued as a popular tradition for over a hundred years, and its renditions were heard far and wide. "Miss Lemay" is a fictional character. Written in the 1950s.

Oh, hear the Mounted Police Band play
To honour Miss Lemay,
They're marching in their scarlet coats
This lovely summer day.
Their buttons bright, the tunics tight,
The Band is on display.
It seems as if they always say,
"Oh, where is Miss Lemay?"

They need a lovely mascot,
And someone for a pet,
And they know without a doubt
She's the sweetest they can get.
They're playing on the courthouse square
Facing all the ladies fair,
Clanging, blowing, beating drums,
For the girl who isn't there!

Now the Police Band has no sweetheart,
Their music is so sad,
So please come back home to Ottawa
Before they all go mad.

Then every Redcoat will be gay,
Hurray for Miss Lemay.
They'll whistle, boom, ta-roo-la-loo,
How happy they would be,
And they will cheer and play real good
For lovely Miss Lemay.

TALL TALES AND TRUE STORIES

The Bootlegger

—A. L. Freebairn

This poem, written circa 1879, is set in Fort Macleod, Alberta (then the Northwest Territories), when prohibition was in force. From Scarlet and Gold *and* Wake the Prairie Echoes.

In the days gone by, when the West was dry,
Back in eighteen seventy-nine,
Old Nosey Ford brought in a load
Of "red-eye" from the line.
He knew right well he'd sure get hell
If the Mounted Force got wise
So a short way back from his old log shack
He cached his merchandise.

Then it seemed each day, in a casual way,
He'd wander down to bring
With an old tin can, just like any man,
Some water from the spring.
But the thirsty knew, and they were not few,
Where the liquor could be got,
And the old blind pig, was going big
At fifty cents a shot.

Till Sergeant Brail of the town detail,
A suspicious sort of guy,
Says, "I'll bet my stripes there's booze by cripes,
In Nosey's—or close by."
So plans were made for a whiskey raid
On the shack at the end of town.
Brail, with some more, knocked on the door,
With a warrant from the Crown.

"Come in, come in, and stop your din,"
Was Nosey's kind invite;
"Just playin' cards with two, three pards
That happened in tonight.
They'll all agree suspectin' me
Is all a lot of bosh;
But search you may, and by the way,
I'll give my hands a wash."

He dumped the can into a pan
And gave himself a wash.
He lathered well, and sure as hell
That man had nerve by gosh.
He threw the suds out in the mud—
Liquor, of course, but could the Force
Still prove it any more?

So ends the tale of the bootleg trail
That led from Whiskey Gap
To Fort Macleod and the old time crowd,
That put it on the map;
For Nosey Ford, with his next big load,
Was caught by Sergeant Brail,
And you bet, by gosh, 'ere he could wash
Was safely locked in jail.

The Squad of One

—Robert J. C. Stead

This is a story of a quick-witted sergeant who captured some toughs all on his own—a job that would have required a whole squad of American lawmen. From Robert Stead's The Empire Builders and Other Poems *(William Briggs, Toronto, 1909), RCMP Quarterly, 1969, and* Wake the Prairie Echoes.

Sergeant Blue of the Mounted Police was a so-so kind of guy;
He swore a bit, and he lied a bit, and he boozed a bit on the sly;
But he held the post at Snake Creek Bend for country and home and God,
And he cursed the worst and forgot the rest—which wasn't the least bit
      odd.

Now the life of the North West Mounted Police breeds an all-round kind
      of man;
A man who can jug a down-south thug when he rushes the red-eye can;
A man who can pray with a dying man, or break up a range stampede—
Such are the men of the Mounted Police, and such are the men they
      breed.

The snow lay deep at the Snake Creek post and deep to east and west,
And the Sergeant made his ten-league beat and settled down to rest
In his two-by-four that they called a "post" where the flag flew overhead,
And he took a look at his monthly mail, and this is the note he read:

"To Sergeant Blue, of the Mounted Police, at the post at Snake Creek Bend,
From U.S. Marshal of County Blank, greetings to you, my friend:
They's a team of toughs give us the slip, though they shot up a couple of
      blokes,
And we reckon they's hid in Snake Creek Gulch, and posin' as farmer
      folks.

"They's as full of sin as a barrel of booze, and as quick as a cat with a gun,
So if you happen to hit their trail, be first to start the fun;
And send out your strongest squad of men and round them up if you can,
For dead or alive we want them here. Yours truly, Jack McMann."

And Sergeant Blue sat back and smiled, "Ho, here is a chance of game!
Folks 'round here have been so good that life is getting tame;
I know the lie of Snake Creek Gulch—where I used to set my traps—
I'll blow out there tomorrow, and I'll bring them in—perhaps."

Next morning Sergeant Blue, arrayed in farmer smock and jeans,
In a jumper sleigh he had made himself, set out for the evergreens
That grow on the bank of Snake Creek Gulch by a homestead shack he
 knew.
And a smoke curled up from the chimney-pipe to welcome Sergeant Blue.

"Aha, and that looks good to me," said the Sergeant to the smoke,
"For the lad that owns this homestead shack is east in his wedding-yoke;
There are strangers here, and I'll bet a farm against a horn of booze
That they are the bums that are predestined to dangle in a noose."

So he drove his horse to the shanty door and hollered a loud "Good-day,"
And a couple of men with fighting-irons came out beside the sleigh,
And the Sergeant said, "I'm a stranger here and I've driven a weary mile;
If you don't object I'll just sit down by the stove in the shack awhile."

Then the Sergeant sat and smoked and talked of the home he had left
 down East,
And the cold and the snow, and the price of land, and the life of man and
 beast,
But all of a sudden he broke it off with, "Neighbours, take a nip,
There's a horn of the best you'll find out there in my jumper, in the grip."

So one of the two went out for it, and as soon as he closed the door,
The other one staggered back as he gazed up the nose of a forty-four;
But the Sergeant wasted no words with him, "Now, fellow, you're on the
 rocks,
And a noise as loud as a mouse from you and they'll take you out in a
 box."

And he fastened bracelets to his wrists, and his legs with some binder
thread
And he took his knife, and he took his gun, and he rolled him on to the
bed;
And then as number two came in, he said, "If you want to live,
Put up your dukes and behave yourself, or I'll make you into a sieve."

And when he had coupled them each to each and laid them out on the
bed,
"It's cold, and I guess we'd better eat before we go," he said.
So he fried some pork and he warmed some beans, and he set out the
best he saw,
And they ate thereof, and he paid for it according to British law.

That night in the post sat Sergeant Blue, with paper and pen in hand,
And this is the word he wrote and signed and mailed to a foreign land,
"To U.S. Marshal of County Blank, greetings I give to you.
My squad has just brought in your men, and the squad was 'Sergeant
Blue.'"

There are things unguessed, there are tales untold, in the life of the great
lone land,
But here is a fact that the prairie-bred alone may understand,
That a thousand miles in the fastness, the fear of the law obtains,
And the pioneers of justice were the "Riders of the Plains."

The Ballad of Macki

—Constable F.E. Torpey, #5314

Mounted patrols for the elusive Macki (which may have been some wily fugitive's nickname) were conducted from "K" Division, Lethbridge, Alberta. Written circa 1915, this poem is also part of the Torpey Papers. From Wake the Prairie Echoes.

The O.C. told the Sergeant,
And told him pretty plain,
"Your orders are to get that man,
And bring him here by train."
Mac-ki ... Mac-Ki ... Mac-Ki ...

So the Sergeant passed the word along,
The "four-nine" parallel.
And soon six cussing Mounties,
Were looking for that swell.
Mac-ki ... Mac-Ki ... Mac-Ki ...

All along the Milky River,
From "Writing" to "Wild Horse"
They watched each ford and coulee,
Where 'twas possible to cross.
Mac-ki ... Mac-Ki ... Mac-Ki ...

They rode by day, they rode by night,
(Vide the detachment diary)
And thus they searched, for days and days,
But never found their quarry.
Mac-ki ... Mac-Ki ... Mac-Ki ...

The O.C. said, "It's funny,
No news from Sergeant Hood.
It's plain to me that not a man,
Down there is any good."
Mac-ki ... Mac-Ki ... Mac-Ki ...

'Twas strange they couldn't find him,
Those six brave Mounties. Oh,
But the reason I must tell you,
Mac was down in Mexico!
Mac-ki ... Mac-Ki ... Mac-Ki ...

Terry McGee

—J.G. Wilson

The theme of the lone policeman combatting the problem of illicit liquor in the Touchwood Hills, Saskatchewan, is presented here. From Lightfoot, Lord of the Mighty Pack and Other Poems *and* Wake the Prairie Echoes.

> Terry McGee was one of the men
> Who rode the rolling plain,
> In the scarlet coat of the Mounted Police,
> As a member of the same.
> His hair was red, his eyes were blue,
> His face a sunburnt tan,
> A native son of the Emerald Isle,
> With a record for getting his man.
>
> He was holding down a lonesome post
> At the foot of the Touchwood Hills,
> His instructions were to peel an eye
> For the smoke of the moonshine stills,
> To locate and seize a crock or two
> Of the reeking mountain brew,
> And to bring to fort by hook or by crook
> The ringleader of the crew.
>
> So Terry had spent a week or so
> In getting the lay of the land,
> 'Til he found that one-eyed Curly Pete
> Was chief of the wanted band.
> He also found that the Touchwood folks
> Were holding their annual ball
> On Thursday night, at eight o'clock
> In the old community hall.

So on Friday night he dressed himself
Like the folks of the Touchwood Hills,
And then he loaded his forty-five,
With some brass-coated iron pills,
While he packed in his hip a pair of cuffs,
That he took from a peg on the wall,
Then he forked his mount and headed north
For the moonshiners' annual ball.

Now Terry McGee was a primitive man
And action was what he liked,
So he schemed his schemes and laid his plans,
As the mountain trail he hiked.
'Til at last the drone of a lone violin
Drifted out on the evening breeze.
Then Terry dismounted and tied his nag
To a bluff of evergreen trees.

He drifted round the old log hall
'Til he stood near the open door,
The music had stopped, and one-eyed
Pete was standing alone on the floor.
His voice was thick with a homebrew lisp
His eye was a bloodshot red,
But he held the crowd with his boastful air
And these were the words he said:

"I've heard today that them red-coated guys
Are sending up here to the hills,
A man of the Force, named Terry McGee,
To try and locate our stills.
He has in his jeans, so I've been told,
A warrant for one-eyed Pete,
If ever we meet, that mounted man
Will die with his boots on his feet.

"For I'm going to get this Terry McGee,
And the getting will just be fun,
Before the smoke's cleared right away
I'll have added a notch to my gun.
A friend of mine down at Wild Cat Creek
Is keeping his eye on the bird,
And when he heads for the Touchwood Hills
He's going to pass the word."

One-eyed Pete had finished his speech
And started to leave the floor
When Terry McGee of the Mounted Police
Stepped in thro' the open door.
He looked the part of a haunted man,
As he glared for a second or two,
Then turning to one-eyed Curly Pete,
He said, "I've a message for you.

"A friend of yours at Wild Cat Creek,
Whom I happened to meet today,
Told me to tell you that Terry McGee
Was bent on heading this way;
So I'll bid you goodnight, tho' I'd rather stay
As my throat is parched and raw,
But I've got to keep hitting the lonesome trail
A jump ahead of the law.

Then one-eyed Pete let an awful whoop,
"Oh, I'm going to have some fun,
You're just the man I'm looking for,
You raw-boned son-of-a-gun,
So you're keeping a jump ahead of the law,
Doggone your rawhide shoes,
Come out with me to my saddle bags
And I'll give you a shot of booze."

So Terry and Pete took a little hike
To a bluff of evergreen trees,
While the violin's drone of "Home, Sweet Home,"
Mixed with the evening breeze.
When Pete produced a crock of booze,
He nearly dropped with surprise,
When held in the hand of Terry McGee
Was a blue-nosed forty-five.

Two riders approached a distant fort,
Some two hours after dawn,
Two voices were mixed with threats untold,
And the lilt of an Irish song.
The man who swore what he would do,
If his hands were only free
Was known as one-eyed Curly Pete,
The singer was Terry McGee.

The Sergeant's Tale of the Manitoba Stonehenge

—Anonymous

The origin of this poem is unknown, but it is a mysterious and compelling tale. It would be interesting to know when and where it was published, if it ever was.

Prologue

The tightest-lipped of all who sat, beside that fire and smoked in peace
Was that steel-jawed aristocrat, the red-coated Sergeant of Police.
So Casey led our talk about, and tried to draw the Sergeant out.
"I've often heard it claimed," he said, "That in the West, since Time began
And Adam's kids began to spread, the Mounties always got their man.
Is it the truth the spalpeens speak, or are their facts a trifle weak?"

Like sunrise on a foggy cliff, the glimmer of a smile awoke
Behind the Sergeant's mighty whiff of eddying tobacco smoke:
"You say the Force is never wrong; but though the Law's red arm is long,
And though few men escape our hand, from Morden north to Baffin Land,
Yet there are cases, I'll admit, that buffalo the boys a bit.
Sometimes sheer luck or Providence, is all that cleans up an offence,
And credit for a crime's solution, comes from uncanny retribution
That overtakes the wicked, when they think their crime unseen by men.

"I call to mind a baffling case, up in the northern mining region,
Back in those first prospecting days, just before Flin Flon brought a legion
Of hard-boiled, strong-arm miners in, to curse the wilderness with din.
Except for Fate, I question whether, the Force had not been bound to fail;
For later, piecing things together, we got a most amazing tale
From the last member of the gang, who died too soon for us to hang."
The Sergeant halted. No one stirred while he lit up a fresh cigar
And went on, weighing every word, to tell how, up in wilds afar, higher
Vengeance came to show, the murder of a sourdough."

I

"Up where the line of travel crosses, from Footprint Lake to Mistowasis,
Two hundred miles from Norway House, northward by portage-trail and
    river,
Where Arctic foxes prowl for grouse, and where the mossy muskegs
    quiver
By moose-ponds lying cool and black, through endless spruce and
    tamarack,
The wealth of milky reefs of quartz, ribbing the wilderness of granite,
Now brings prospectors of all sorts, who hope for gold and come to scan
    it.
Twelve years ago, before the rush, three sourdoughs, one summer day,
Came by canoe, their brows a-flush, with hope that fortune might repay,
Their present toil a hundredfold with rich discoveries of gold.
Bill Smith, Jack Lloyd, and Pete MacLeod, these unkempt, bearded sons
    of Chance,
Had left The Pas beneath a cloud of most suspicious circumstance,
And fogs of dark unproven blame, arising from a poker game.
Deserved or not, bad fortune dogged them: a storm on Lake Athapapuskow
Upset their boat and muskeg bogged them, along a trail near Lake
    Wekusko;
Most of their grub-stake thus was gone, but still they struggled grimly on;
Hoping to reimburse their losses, by striking gold near Mistowasis.
Fly-time was at its very worst: out of dank woods and bogs accurst,
Blood-hungry blackflies came to fare, behind their ears and in their hair,
While yellow-banded moose-flies bit, raising red welts where'er they lit,
And thick mosquito clouds would drone a maddening, murderous
    monotone.

"But blood-gorged pests and rations' shortage, were for a moment quite
    forgot
When the men sighted at a portage, a big bull-moose, a perfect shot.
Pete raised his rifle silently, but the mere movement stirred the bull
To turn for flight past rock and tree, just as his finger crooked to pull.
The rifle barked. The great beast lurched, then lumbered off. 'I've hit the
    brute!
Come on!' And eagerly they searched through jackpine thickets, where
    his route

Lay clear in hoof prints in the mud, with broken twigs and flecks of blood.
Then, on a sudden rocky slope, they found the moose, whose blood's
    dark streams
Dabbled the quartz-reef of their hope, the golden outcrop of their dreams!
Ten rods to left and right it spread, that broad, white vein with gold
    encrusted,
And the great beast there, lying dead, was naught to this, for which they
    lusted
With all the raw, primeval greed, of gamblers in their time of need.
Kneeling there, joyous beyond measure, they gloated on their new-found
    treasure."

II

"Two evenings later found them camped, far back upon the homeward
    trail.
By portage shortcuts they had tramped, with their canoe, intent to scale,
The brief, abrupt, basalt divide, out to the Nelson River side
And with all haste record their names, in Winnipeg, to clinch their claims.
At nightfall, glad to break their trudge, they camped and sheltered by a
    smudge
From ravenous mosquito-hosts; they ate fried moose and made their
    boasts,
How they would live in highest pitch, of revelry when they were rich.

"Then, by ill fortune, Pete MacLeod took from his battered dunnage pack
A crock of whiskey, and he vowed he wouldn't wait till he got back:
'Now is the time for celebration, I am so dry, I know right well
I'd face the Devil and damnation, just for a drink!' And all three fell
To boozing in a noisy choir, around their murky little fire.
Then, as the fumes of whiskey mounted, up from the belly to the brains,
Drunk Jack to drunken Bill recounted, how much more rich would be
    their gains
If they should stab drunk Peter through, and share the mine between the
    two.
'Listen,' he whispered to his mate, 'Get out your skinning-knife, and wait:
And while he snores beside his pack, we'll stab the rascal in the back.'
Such was their deed, but hands unsteady, wounded but did not kill their
    man.

Up leapt poor Pete, half-slain already by streaming wounds, and
staggering, ran
Along a little forest path, while after him, in drunken wrath,
His comrades, each with dripping knife, came lurching on to take his life."

III

"Wan moonlight lit the path they took; and haggard Pete in hopeless
terror
Soon slackened pace, with knees that shook, for he had stumbled in his
error,
Into the weirdest rocky glen, e'er gazed upon by mortal men.
Hemmed in by high, sheer walls of black, steep as the ramparts of a
crater,
A treeless rocky pit stretched back, shaped like a grave but vastly greater,
And on its phosphorescent floor, some human tribe of ages gone
Had ranged huge boulders by the score, to form a giant skeleton,
A Manitoba Stonehenge, set with symbolism grimmer yet.
Into that pit, Pete sickly gazed. The butchering pair were close behind
him,
And on he staggered, horror-crazed: down in that gulch they might not
find him.
But soon he sank upon the stones, beside those vast, symbolic bones,
Exhausted, and with swimming eyes, looked at his slaughterous allies.
'Dead men,' said Bill, 'are slow to quote, especially after due cremation.'
And drew his knife across Pete's throat, with murderous deliberation.
'Now let us build a fire,' he said. 'The blasted gulch is off the trail.
We'll burn this rascal who is dead, and not a trace will tell his tale.
When we get back to Winnipeg, we'll say he drowned in Fiddle Lake;
And not a person there will beg, for further details for his sake.'

"Under the wan, uncanny moon, they dragged down wood into the chasm;
Pete crackled on his pyre soon, but Jack Lloyd almost took a spasm
When by the light of that foul fire, a tall, dark stranger seemed to stand
Among the stones beside the pyre, and hail them with uplifted hand.
He looked like some old Indian priest, and towered nine feet high at least;
And when he spoke, his accents fell, like organ music played in Hell:
'Do not expect,' he said to Bill, 'to go unpunished for your crime.

Though human law prove not your ill, yet rest assured that in due time,
You, who have merited such blame, shall perish here in penal flame;
And your ally shall earn his hire, on lingering death, but not by fire.'
But Bill in drunk derision cursed: 'I'll see you on this bonfire first!'
And a wild rain of slugs were dealt, from the revolver at his belt.
As moon and firelight seemed to dim, they saw the stranger's form
    dislimb,
And fade among the mammoth bones; and all they found among the
    stones
Were half a dozen tiny pocks."

IV

"Five years passed by. The death of Pete by drowning had been put to
    question,
But all our efforts met defeat. There was no corpse. And the suggestion
That something was extremely wrong, was proofless, though belief was
    strong.

"Meanwhile the mine at Mistowasis, was pouring out a golden store,
Of bullion for its two grim bosses, and still they darkly craved for more.
Air transport companies had brought, to loot that shining reef of quartz,
All of the tools that modern thought has fashioned: there were sundry
    sorts,
Of stamp mills and amalgamators, each with its own peculiar failings,
With mercury in stamp-box crates, and cyanide for slime, and tailings;
And towering mounds of refuse rose, where Pete MacLeod had trailed
    that moose,
While the incessant stamp-mill blows, rang through the silent miles of
    spruce.
Since neither road nor railway ran, into this realm of Smith and Lloyd,
And since the plant—machine and man—had come on wings across the
    void,
Bill Smith, who frequently had flown, soon bought a biplane of his own,
And having earned his pilot's papers, grew constant in his airy capers.
One August morning, he and Jack had put in eighteen holes of golf
At Deer Lodge, before starting back to see the mine. The pair took off
Just as the air-field clock struck noon; at full speed they expected soon,

To cross five hundred miles of sky, to where the mine would cheer their
    eye.
But engine trouble held them stalled at Norway House for several hours;
And to Jack Lloyd, Bill seemed enthralled by dark, infuriating Powers:
His tongue lolled like a dog's in drought, his bloodshot eyes were wild
    and staring,
And nervous twitchings at the mouth, made his fierce glance seem yet
    more glaring;
While his remarks, as day decreased, seemed like the snarls of some wild
    beast,
The long, slow twilight of the North, had merged with darkness when at
    last
The plane was ready to set forth; and as the light was fully past,
Jack urged it would be wise to stay at Norway House till break of day.

"'You coward!' Bill began to mock. 'The moon comes up at ten o'clock,
Just past the full and plenty bright, to show our way across the night.
You'll get into that plane, you blackguard, or learn how lead can cure a
    laggard!'
More nervous over Bill's wild mood than any hazards of the dark,
And feeling that some trouble brewed, from a mad fit so strange and stark,
Jack, in slow silence, got on board; and just at moonrise, off they soared.
A sea of shadows lay below them, silvered with soft, unearthly light.

"Only vague outlines served to show them, their northward way across
    the night.
Onward they hurtled, flying low; when suddenly Jack's blood ran cold—
For there before them, all aglow, with hellish glare as bright as gold,
A sunken, treeless valley shone, upon whose floor, outlined with fires,
A grim titanic skeleton, leered upward at the gaping fliers.
'That is the place you murdered Pete!' said Jack to Bill. 'No, it was you,'
He answered with demented heat: 'Who killed the rascal? Tell me, who?'
Just at that moment, from the gloom, a huge, white owl, with skull-like
    eyes,
Swooped like a messenger of doom, and with infuriated cries
Of 'Who? Who? Who?' attacked the pair. Bill lost control, and through the
    air,
Fell yelling with the twisting plane. Jack leapt out clear. Bill tried in vain,
With parachute too badly tangled. The plane took fire. Alive but mangled,

He perished screeching in the fire, near where the ashes of Pete's pyre
Still lingered, hideous, moist and grey, though five long years had passed
   away.
We learned all this next day, for Jack bailed out too low and broke his
   back,
But lingered long enough to tell the truth about their deed of hell.
Fire rangers who had sighted a sudden, flaming plane come down,
Went there at dawn, looked and alighted, and flew me promptly in from
   town.

"Much of the tale is hard to credit, but though the yarn is weird and gory,
It was a dying man who said it, and he believed his own dark story;
And when we found charred bones of Pete, the bloody record seemed
   complete,
Proving, as said when I began, that Fate can help us get our man."

The Corporal's Tale of the Men Who Vanished

—Anonymous

Like the previous poem, the origin of this one is unknown. Another intriguing tale, its narrative style suggests it may be by the same author.

Prologue

The lean-faced Corporal nodded slow, his confirmation of the tale:
"Yes," he remarked, "I also know a case where Heaven did not fail
To interpose its Justice, when a ruthless pair of wicked men
Transgressed the laws of man and God. But if the Sergeant's case was
    odd,
This one, I think, was weirder still. Let me rehearse the tale of ill."
We puffed approval, though unneeded, and the gaunt Corporal proceeded:

I

"The precious pair of whom I spoke were 'One-eyed Mike' and 'Scarface
    Dan,'
As reckless, evil-hearted folk as ever harried mortal man.
Perhaps some thugs are still more black, like those chill connoisseurs in
    crime
Who send your kidnapped children back, one severed finger at a time;
But Mike and Dan were beasts at best. There were no worse in all the
    West,
Both were Bulgarians by birth; as youths they had been jailed for murder,
And might have hanged and slept in earth, had not a policy absurder
Than all unreason being fed, by bounties of so much a head
For western settlers in the raw, transferred them out to Canada.
By just such tactics of perdition, Canadian agents earned commission,
And left the sequel for our nation, to bear in bitter tribulation.
Mike was a stocky sort of guy, with glances fiery as a rocket,
Though through a fight, his fierce left eye was missing wholly from its
    socket.
Dan, unlike Mike, was lean and bleak, with grizzled stubble on his chin,
And a long scar across his cheek that gave him an unearthly grin.

157

After six months of pioneering, up near The Pas, they tired of clearing
And faded out to Winnipeg, where each soon flourished as a yegg.
Then, when police hunts grew too hot, they sought a less frequented spot,
And hit on a deserted shack, out in the Rockies, north of Yahk."

II

"From this new base of operations, they started on fresh depredations,
And often vexed with thievish sally, the humble Slovaks of the valley.
Emboldened by the latter's mildness, they soon went on to greater
    wildness,
And dared one Sabbath day to search, and rob the entire Slovak church.
The priest was halfway through the Mass, when the two Bulgars, bold as
    brass,
A six-gun poised in either hand, came striding in, with sharp command,
To face the walls and raise their arms; then, breathing threats of grievous
    harms,
They quickly took, with ribald mirth, all each possessed of any worth.
Mike's one fierce eye was full of scorn, and Dan's scarred grin was bleak
    and pale,
Watching the old priest stand forlorn, beside the little altar rail.
He lifted up his hand; and lo, the pair, who were about to go,
Halted in silence as his wrath, burst in a thundering aftermath.
He cursed their souls to lowest hell; he cursed their worthless flesh as
    well;
He cursed their waking hours with pain; he cursed their sleep with
    horror's reign;
He cursed their skins with tick and louse; he cursed the safety of their
    house,
'On you shall surely come,' he cried, 'a far worse fate than if you died.
With all your human senses keen, you shall subsist on food obscene,
And snarl and howl with beastly breath, in anguished eagerness for death.
Within this day your work of sin, its penal torment shall begin.
Go! Or, before it is too late, kneel down and pray for your sad state.'"

III

"Giving a laugh, the scornful pair strode out and left him standing there,
Mounted their nags and rode away, and called it a successful day.

Of this affair we Mounties heard, for several weeks no single word;
For Slovak folk, devoutly odd, preferred to leave such things to God,
And saw no need to tell the police, about such breaches of the peace.
At length the Winnipeg command, trailed the two miscreants to the land,
And one day I rode out from Yahk, to seize the men and bring them back.
Then, at the village in the valley, the old priest told me stoically,
About the Sunday when his flock were rudely robbed and set at mock,
Yet said there was no need to send, for villains who had met their end;
No one had seen them since that time; God, he was sure, had marked
    their crime,
And had pleased on them to vent, unprecedented punishment.

"When I insisted on my ride, he sent a Slovak as my guide,
Who, with his face a trifle pale, soon led me up the mountain trail.
It was a bleak November day, as we rode up that rugged way.
Borne by a piercing autumn wind, grey clouds in drifting ribbons thinn'd
Across tall crags of naked stone, that shone as cold as polished bone,
And colder still behind them rose, fantastic summits white with snow.
I am not a religious sort, yet I can candidly report,
I sensed upon that mountain path, God's purity and awful wrath."

IV

"Around a corner of the trail, we met the cabin suddenly,
A wooden shack, unkempt and frail, beneath a thunder-smitten tree,
A pine whose green had turned instead to haggard, fateful hues of red.
A battered stable stood behind it, in ruinous dilapidation;
As with the house, we seemed to find it a thing of utter desolation.
Hemmed round by shining peaks of morning, they lay beneath a sense of
    night,
As if the spot, in awful warning, were smitten by some nameless blight.
The shack's one door was open wide, upon a sagging pair of hinges,
And as we slowly stepped inside, I felt my hair roots stir with twinges
Of some unutterable awe, scarce called for by the thing I saw.

"For little was there to be seen in that uncanny, dusty room
Two empty beds, a stove unclean, two upturned chairs, a broken broom,
Two suits of clothes, half-torn to shreds, that lay on the dishevelled beds,
And on a table, neatly stacked, as if to satisfy our search,

The booty we had duly tracked, the plunder of the Slovak church.
And then I saw, with one glance more, that all along the cabin floor,
Were countless wolf tracks in the dust, and marks where, in some fierce
 disgust,
Wild teeth and claws, their frenzy spreading, had gnawed the bed and
 clawed the bedding.
But of the Bulgars, Mike and Dan, no single sign was there to scan,
Yes, though we searched on every side, we could not find them, hair nor
 hide,
Nor even bloodstains anywhere, to show that wolves had killed them
 there.
Here were their clothes, and fruits of theft, but the two men themselves
 had left,
And, without leaving any trace, had simply vanished into space.
Going out back to search the shed, we found its door was open too,
And there, repulsive to the view, two saddle-horses, long since dead,
Were lying on the earthen floor, while at their mangled haunches tore,
Two mangy wolves, two cringing beasts, who seemed to loathe such
 carrion feasts.
Then, as I made a sudden sound, the wretched creatures turned around,
In snarling anger to unsheathe, from haggard lips their yellow teeth.
I drew my gun. The Slovak checked me, and crossed himself in pious awe.
Then, with his finger to direct me, the thicker, stockier brute I saw
Had glances fiery as a rocket, and one eye missing from its socket,
While his companion wolf was bleak, lean as the famine-curst are thin,
With a long scar across his cheek, that gave him an unearthly grin.
They did not fight but only cowered, back in the corner of a stall;
And there I left them as they glowered, and did not harm the brutes at
 all."

V

"I'm sure my face was very pale, as we rode back along the trail;
At any rate, I know my mind was reeling, and I could not find,
An answer to the uncanny sights, up at that homestead on the heights.
Under the cold November skies, beneath those awful mountain summits,
I thought of a man as one who dies, a feeble beast, whose reason
 plummets,

Over the surface of a sea, of spiritual mystery.
What I had seen I scarce could tell, yet somehow knew a moving swell,
From holy seas beyond my ken, had washed the sin-stained shores of
men,
And sweeping up along the beach, had touched a spot beyond the reach
Of common tides and common reason, to punish evil in its season.

"Yet when I turned in my police report, I gave no version of that sort.
My humble Slovak guide and I could never hope to satisfy
A Philistine intelligence, with tales that somehow had no sense.
So to my chief I merely said: 'The men are missing, likely dead.
We found the homestead wolf-infested; no doubt the pair are now
digested.'
That's what I told him. But I know, that after all it wasn't so,
And that it was my privilege, to stand upon the outer edge
Of a stupendous mystery, beyond the guess of you and me."

TRIBUTES TO THE FORCE AND ITS VETERANS

Toast to the Vets

—Eleanor (Andres) Wafler

The author, wife of J.A. Wafler, #17097, presented this poem in 1996 as a toast at an RCMP veterans' Annual General Meeting dinner banquet.

You've reached your time of well-earned rest,
For many years you've done your best,
To maintain the "right" as you were told,
Worked towards pension when you got old.

Well, times have changed, these many years,
Your duties were filled with blood, sweat and tears,
Work days were long and pay was meagre,
To earn a stripe—you all were eager.

Remember when you'd go to work,
With brass buttons polished and a starched, ironed shirt?
Brown serge so snug, you could barely breathe,
Boots laced so tight, you dared not sneeze.

You'd walk the beat and try each door,
Afraid to enter an unlocked store,
When punks were mouthy, it became quite plain,
They needed an education in some dark lane.

The courts were saved both time and money,
To mess with a cop, they found, wasn't funny.
To marry back then was another task,
"Your obedient servant" for permission did ask.

First ten, then seven, then five years, then three,
You had to serve loyally, before matrimony.
You had to be totally out of debt,
And your assets $1200 must net.

This helped to furnish our first abode,
But covered crates and steamer trunk were also in vogue.
You'd slip home for lunch in "the" police car,
Park near an open window—never too far.

To hear a call on the radio,
Leave your meal—or eat on the go.
Many were stationed in an isolated place,
Where office and living quarters shared the same space.

Wives took calls and helped their men,
Cooked meals for prisoners
And never knew when
Their lives would be threatened.

Cool heads did prevail,
Many ladies here could tell a golden tale.
Remember the prisoners who were in your care?
Sunday morning they'd do their share.

Like cutting the lawn, and washing your car,
You watched diligently that they didn't stray far,
'Twould be embarrassing to say,
"Sorry Sir—they got away."

When on parade and dressed in red,
You turned many a young girl's head,
They'd ask to take a picture with you,
There was nothing we poor wives could do.

So now you are here, very much alive,
Many have gone, but you have survived,
You didn't think you'd see the day
That women would earn equal pay.

The turban is part of your uniform,
In time we all will have to conform.
They have twelve-hour shifts, with four days of rest,
An association to back them, it's one of the best.

They wear bomber jackets and loose-fitting shirts,
No hats in cars, they've changed the works.
Now there are brawls and riots galore,
Respect for the law has gone out the door.

If you had your choice, I think you'd say,
"I'm glad I am where I am at today."
And now—you're still our handsome men,
Standing proud and straight as you did then.

Even though your hair has turned to grey,
We love and salute our "Vets" today.

The Love of My Life

—Elizabeth (Brunet) Thibeault, Maple Bay, British Columbia

Mrs. Thibeault expresses love and admiration for her late husband, Superintendent J.W. Maurice Thibeault, who was originally from the small northern town of La Tuque, Québec. Maurice was an excellent officer who passed away in December 1992. He was also my brother-in-law: we married sisters in a double RCMP wedding in Ottawa, Ontario, in October 1960.

I met him in the springtime,
By autumn I'd claimed him as mine.
Taller than the tallest tree,
This is what he meant to me.
So handsome, gentle, warm and dear,
A man of the law who displayed no fear.

He wore the glorious gold and red,
The day my "Mountie" and I were wed.
What joy, and oh, what pride,
When he stood close by my side.

I replied "I will" and promised my love,
God was surely smiling from above.
Our wedded years were full beyond compare,
They said that we made such a loving pair.

One day God took him to his heavenly home,
My heart was crushed—I felt so alone.
But time has eased my dreadful pain
And now there is meaning in my life again.
I know he hears my prayers for help
For I feel a greater strength within myself.

The Veterans—Silent Are the Brave

—R.W. (Bob) Morley, #14863, Courtenay, British Columbia

A fine tribute to those who did their duty well. Morley wrote the poem in 1997 especially for this anthology.

In the misty shrouds of Valhalla—that kingdom of the dead,
Darkened shrines and hushed salutes to heroes gone ahead;
As fearlessly they broke our trail,
No faltering steps to their Holy Grail.

From east to west they followed their stern and silent guide
For hours of bleak monotony, then danger on every side;
The only law on a lonely night,
On a lonely trail because it's right.

If you have never travelled in danger's way you will never know,
Desperate men who play deadly games can deal a mortal blow;
They don't know your number, rank, or name,
But they will kill you, to hell with blame.

Old heroes will never turn away, an ancient law they must enforce,
"Maintain The Right" says it all, but has deadly fortune run its course?
To be brave there's but a single test,
Just face them down and do your best.

Their friends have ridden westward, boots and saddles to the sun,
They faced their maker, they did their best, now their battle's run;
For there's something in a veteran's stride,
He's proud because he knows he tried.

When they meet they'll raise a glass and toast an absent friend,
A silent gesture to their dead, old friends who met their end.
They smile for only they know the story,
Of law, and right, and an old Mountie's glory.

They did their duty well, those scarlet riders of the sky,
They passed the colours on to younger hands, flag still flying high
Now together but alone they turn away with pride
And to their own Valhalla, softly, silently ride.

Reason for Late Dues

—J.A.L. Foster, #15176, Nanaimo, British Columbia

Printed in Regina Division's RCMP Veterans' Bulletin in 1997. Just a little humour.

Just a line to say I'm living,
That I'm not among the dead;
Though I'm getting more forgetful
And mixed up in the head.

I got used to my arthritis,
To my dentures I'm resigned.
I can manage my bifocals,
But God, I miss my mind.

For sometimes I can't remember, when
I stand at the foot of the stairs,
If I must go up for something
Or have I just come down from there?

And before the fridge, so often
My poor mind is filled with doubt;
Have I just put food away
Or have I come to take some out?

And there's times when it is dark,
With my nightcap on my head,
I don't know if I'm retiring
Or just getting out of bed.

So, if it's my time to pay you
There's no need for getting sore
I may think that I have remitted
And I don't want to be a bore.

Here I stand beside the mail box
With a face so very red;
Instead of mailing you this letter
I had opened it instead.

Rhyme of the Ancient Mounted Man

—Anonymous

Modelled after Coleridge's Rime of the Ancient Mariner, *this amusing poem, written in the 1940s, talks about how police duties have evolved over the years (with a few exaggerations).*

It was an Ancient Mounted Man
And he stopped one of three,
A pink-cheeked youth in a Stetson hat
And boots laced to the knee.

In a chocolate coat with a maiden's belt
A cravat of silk, dyed blue,
The kid was peeved at the old man's gall
And from his clutch withdrew.

The greybeard raised his skinny hand
"There was a time," quoth he,
"Shut up, and beat it, dodd'ring loon
No hot-air yarns for me."

He held him with his glitt'ring eye
The R.C. buck stood still,
And listened like a three-years' child
The old chap had his will.

The R.C. youth sat on a stone,
He had no guts to flee,
And thus spoke on that ancient man
Of the Royal North West MP.

"There was a time when we served for fun
And a 'four-bit' touch for pay."
"Is that so?" sniffed the pink-cheeked one
"I'm paid two planks per day!"

"The murd'rer quailed when we started out
To end his career of sin,
And the horse thief spurred his mount in vain,
He was always gathered in.

"We patrolled from the Line to the frozen North
And we kept the Public Peace;
Now tell me, boy, of your job today
In the R.C. Mounted Police."

The pink-cheeked youth hid a wearied yawn
"That horse-thief stuff's absurd;
It's an easier job to enforce the law
Re the Migratory Bird.

"And if one wants to divert one's mind
With something more serene,
There's Memo number Two-Eight-Four
Re Oleo Margarine.

"The Act re Inland Revenue
Just brings one joy in jugs;
And for a change we've the law re Hop
And all Narcotic Drugs.

"And I mustn't forget the OBU
You know how we saved the nation?
You should hear us quiz the applicant
For Nat-ur-al-i-za-tion."

The old man raised his skinny hand
And bade the youth to cease;
"Ah—thus it was not in the days
Of the North West Mounted Police.

"We knew not Oleo Margarine
Nor OBUs nor Drugs;
We rode the Plains and we rid the Plains
Of Murd'rers, Thieves, and Thugs.

"We cared no whit for Revenue
Nor Migrate birds that lay;
We did Police work, and did it right
For Fifty Cents per day.

"Farewell, farewell, but this I tell
To thee—without bombast;
We were paid well who served so well
The country in the past.

"But he's paid best who serveth best
The Moguls way down East;
The great high powers who own us all
Man, Kit, and Saddle Beast."

The Ancient One whose eyes were bright,
Whose beard with age was hoar
Was gone, and now a weary youth
Entered the canteen door.

He purchased chocolate bars and gum
He quaffed his Lemon Sour;
And wondered how that Ancient Loon
Had held him for an hour.

Pensioned

—J.E. Hungerford

From Enginemen's Magazine *and* RCMP Quarterly, *1947.*

> They gave of their love and their labour;
> They gave of their courage and skill;
> They gave to their less fortunate neighbour,
> And cheerfully footed the bill!
>
> Their work, they gave faithful attention,
> The best that was in them to give,
> And now they are drawing a pension,
> A pension, as long as they live.
>
> They were friends to their brothers about them,
> They were there, when a "pal" was in need,
> And the world would be poorer without them,
> For they lived by the Golden Rule creed!
>
> In their work, they were faithful, unswerving,
> Gave all that was in them to give,
> And their pension they're really deserving,
> And our love, as long as they live!

Ode to the Mounties

—Jack Lidgett, Fir Mountain, Saskatchewan

First printed in Le Lingot du Saguenay, *Arvida, Québec, 1947. From* Wake the Prairie Echoes.

The Mounties. Yes, that word we know,
From school days to the end of our days,
Some will say, "Why is that so?"
Read your history then you will know
Why the saying goes, "They always get their man."
In crime or succour, it's the same to them.

Their duty to do, their faith retain
In the corps we know as the red-coated men.
It may be in the city or the wilds of the north,
On the treeless plain or the prairie so vast,
Some fellow's gone bad and the law defied;
So the Mounties are called to take over the case.

Justice to serve, protection provide
To the people who wish to live a straight life.
History will tell of their record so clear
In cases that made history the world o'er.
Yet sometimes we hear folks say,
"We do not need them today."

That may be the hope of outlaw and bad man as well,
Who know their record, as told in the past,
Their man to get what'er the odds;
To the red-coat men we say, "Carry On."
We know your worth to country and life,
In the wilds of the north or the plains of the south.

Mounties' Reputation

—Betty Kay

The Mounties continue to enjoy an excellent reputation worldwide in the field of policing. Written in 1946.

They are the men of the frozen north,
They are the men of the rolling plains,
The men who protect our Canada
In boats, in cars, in airplanes.

They are the living symbol of honour,
The true north, strong and free,
Ever loyal, and on the alert,
To Canada and our sovereignty.

They ask no fame or publicity,
No matter how perilous a mission,
Their goal has been set with efficiency,
That goal of undying tradition.

They are a force worldwide known
For their stubbornness to do or die.
Let England have her Scotland Yard,
And the United States her FBI.

For no other race throughout the world,
No matter how strong the nation,
Will ever create such a group of men,
As to exceed the Mounties' reputation.

So the Royal Canadian Mounted Police,
In that distinguished scarlet coat,
Is the world's best force of law and order,
Beyond a shadow of a doubt.

A Knock on the Door

—Edith Fullner

Written in the 1940s, this poem expresses a citizen's appreciation for the help of the RCMP.

'Twas a stormy night after a summer's day,
In the Canadian Rockies far away.
I sat alone with trembling and fear,
And not a soul for miles was near.

From crag to crag, thunder dashed,
Jupiter in his fury the heavens slashed,
The pine trees sighed with the element,
Like a million souls in torment.

And then a "Mounted" came
To seek shelter from the storm and rain,
Although I live a hundred years or more,
I'll never forget that welcome knock on the door.

Ere You Partake

—Anonymous

An unknown gentleman left this poem, written in 1919, at a farewell banquet held that year for Sergeant Hubert Thorn, RNWMP, in Edmonton, Alberta. Thorn was the parka-clad mounted policeman who posed for the noted painting by Franz Johnson, showing the end of a trail as a policeman stands over a criminal lying in the snow. From Wake the Prairie Echoes.

> Ere you partake of this most tempting feast,
> To one and all, the greatest and the least,
> I wish a real good time; let each forget
> The daily tasks, which sometimes chafe or fret,
> Let each do well, both old and young,
> The brave deeds of the past oft told and sung;
> And let their memory uplift, inspire,
> And kindle in each heart one great desire
> To emulate those heroes who have gone,
> Your actions take from those who still march on.
>
> Remember brave Fitzgerald and his band,
> Who marched to death at duty's stern command;
> And drink to Sergeant Harper, who you know,
> And Constable Sylvester who through the snow,
> O'er trails, unbroken and new,
> Journeyed afar, but brought his prisoners through;
> Barker, O'Neill, Ritchie, local men,
> Who fought through suffocating smoke, and then
> Removed fourteen male prisoners and two maids
> To safety, count them with the unafraids.
>
> All glory and all honour to the brave,
> Those deeds will speak from out the silent grave,
> And "Duty First," let the old watchword be,
> Forever yours, RNWMP.

Men of the Mounted

—Constable Hugh Riley, #7709

More praise for those men of "sterling worth." Circa 1920s.

Men of the Mounted are put to every test,
Carefully selected, for they must be the best,
Canada feels proud of those men of sterling worth,
The boys in the Scarlet and Gold.

In rebellions of the past they were there until the last,
At the call to arms, they're ever in the fray,
North West Mounted Police, their prestige has increased,
They're the Royal Canadian Mounted of today.

Up in the Arctic or down on the plain,
Ever on duty, keeping laws that are sane,
Respected and honoured the same as of old,
Good luck to the boys in the Scarlet and Gold.

RCMP Memorial Cairn

—Niels Peterson

This short tribute is inscribed on a rock cairn at Glenfair, British Columbia, in memory of three constables killed in the line of duty on June 18, 1962. They were: D.G. Weisgerber, #20215, G.E. Pedersen, #20865, and E.J. Keck, #19233. From Wake the Prairie Echoes.

Pause, stranger, here by this memorial cairn
And bow your head in silence to its beauty,
This sacred monument which tells our brain
Of those who met their fate in line of duty.

From sea to sea, across this mighty land,
From Arctic regions to our southern border,
Such gallant men have taken up their stand
And sacrificed their lives for law and order.

So let this be our tribute to these men,
These gentle men of courage and of vision,
With love that freely flows from heart to pen,
Upholders of an old and proud tradition.

Trumpeter Sounds "Reveille"

—Reverend Edwin H. Knowles, Chaplain, RCMP

Reverend Knowles, who wrote this poem in the 1940s, was also bishop of Qu'Appelle, Saskatchewan. From RCMP Quarterly.

> The saints of God! Their conflict past,
> And life's long battle won at last,
> No more they need the shield or sword,
> They cast them down before the Lord:
> O' happy saints, for ever blest,
> At Jesus' feet how safe you rest.
>
> The saints of God! Their wandering done,
> No more their weary course they run,
> No more they faint, no more they fall,
> No foes oppress, no fears appal,
> O' happy saints, for ever blest,
> In that dear home how sweet your rest.
>
> The saints of God! Life's voyage o'er,
> Safe landed on that blissful shore,
> No stormy tempests now they dread,
> No roaring billows lift their head:
> O' happy saints, for ever blest,
> In that calm haven of your rest.

An RCM Police Anthem

—Anonymous

From riders of the plains to Canada's guardians from sea to sea. Written in the 1950s.

> Our watchword is "Maintain the Right"
> Traditions that can never cease,
> Scarlet-clad, we are proud to be
> Royal Canadian Mounted Police.
>
> The Force marched forth in 'seventy four,
> When Canada's west was wild,
> To bring justice to all men, white or red,
> And see their rights were not defiled.
>
> Since then our men have served,
> Far across the Dominion wide
> Forging those deathless annals
> Which are the Force's pride.
>
> We police the prairie farmlands,
> The shores of the Atlantic main,
> Servants of our countrymen
> Peace and law to maintain.
>
> Our trails in the frozen Arctic,
> Cover many lonely mile,
> We serve on Manitoba's plains
> And fair Prince Edward Isle.
>
> The Klondike's wilds know our men,
> Pacific Coast's verdant strand,
> Upholding our Force's honour,
> Whilst serving our native land.

Those who went on before us,
Passed on their glorious name,
Valiant men and true were they,
Strive to emulate their fame.

We ask no raise or favour,
From those laws we defend
The thought of duty rightly done
Makes us endure to the end.

RCMP Centennial 1973

—J.A. Johnson, #19649, Regina, Saskatchewan

The author of this tribute to the force is proud and happy that he was on hand for the centennial celebrations in 1973 and wrote this poem in 1997 especially for this anthology.

As a member of the RCMP in 1973,
I look back to see what the year meant to me.
Commercially, many people enjoyed a success,
But, this tends to make a birthday party a bit of a mess.

For a police force to survive 100 years,
Calls for gratitude, respect and public cheers.
I was proud to be a member in the Centennial Year,
Of a Force my fellow men started and I cherish so dear.

The Consecration of the New Guidon was a sight to see,
Held at "Depot" Division, Regina, July 4, 1973.
Many key figures were on hand,
Foremost being Her Majesty Queen Elizabeth II and her husband.

Our commissioner and officers from across our country
Helped make this a memorable day for me.
Followed by a banquet later in the day,
And then to see her Majesty on her way.

Photos, coins and many other souvenirs
I obtained and will look back on in the coming years.
It will be impossible for me to see the second centenary,
But, maybe it will be the luck of another member of my family tree.

My son will be told what this year meant to me,
And maybe he will join—I will wait and see.
Weighing the good with the bad,
I was part of 1973, and I am glad.

A Mountie's Last Parade

—B.F. Nowell, #18794, Regina, Saskatchewan

An ode to a fallen comrade. The author intends this poem to be recited at RCMP funerals, if appropriate. He thought of the parade square at Depot Division, Regina, which was the focal point for training, discipline, and decorum. It was the spot where recruits first set foot on that historic ground, and from where they later graduated. Deceased comrades are borne from the RCMP chapel across the square to their final resting place, a most fitting honour.

Come to the square in the morning,
When the dew-wetted breezes blow,
When the troops have polished and paraded
And away to their duties go.

Return to the square in the aft'noon,
When the clear prairie sun is high,
When the worthy day is waning
And a cloud's in the western sky.

Come in the frost of winter,
Or the mellow melt of spring,
Return when the gold of autumn
Is claiming all living thing.

March to the Mounties' Chapel,
Where we shone in our youth and prayed,
His House—where a Mountie is immortal,
Where our history preserves through the age.

Say a prayer, sing a song, then join us
On our last parade 'cross the square
At our graveside, search out the faces
Familiar, gathered round you there.

We will rest, and you'll keep the memories
Of the one who has marched to the tune,
Smile, loved ones and friends, with assurance,
We'll meet in the promised land, soon.

Sunset

—Constable B.G. Boutilier, #14670, RCMP "Marine" Division

*This tribute to the grandeur and beauty of nature provides a fine ending to this
anthology. From* RCMP Quarterly, *1951.*

I stood one eve at sunset, looking out across the bay,
As the breeze was slowly dying, at the closing of the day;
And the gentle, lapping wavelets, washed the seashore at my feet,
While a soft red glow was spreading, where the sky and ocean meet.

All the beauty that is nature, seemed to grow and magnify,
And I gazed in awesome wonder, as it spread across the sky;
All the colours of the rainbow, every tint and every hue,
From the flashing red of fire, to the softest shades of blue.

And the splendour of this sunset, gripped and held me like a spell,
For the story of such beauty, human tongue can never tell;
So I stood serene and peaceful, in the quiet evening hush,
Gazing westward to the heavens, where the Master plied His brush.

GLOSSARY

Place Names

Aklavik Post: On the Mackenzie River delta in the Northwest Territories, this was the headquarters of the Western Arctic sub-district.

Arctic Red River: A small NWMP base about 100 kilometres south of Aklavik, just south of the Arctic Circle.

Bytown: Former name for Ottawa, and location of national RCMP headquarters since 1920.

Cawnpore: "Cawnpore" became the rallying cry for vengeful British troops in colonial India after an uprising there against the British led to a massacre in 1857.

Cypress Hills: Located in present-day Saskatchewan and Alberta, this was the site of a massacre by drunk American wolf hunters upon an innocent (though equally drunk) group of Assiniboine Natives. The incident hastened Prime Minister John A. Macdonald's determination to bring order to Canada's western territory.

Fort Benton: A supply and communications post "as far north as you could go" on the Missouri River, in northern Montana territory. Many things came through here, hence the "Benton Mail."

Fort Dufferin: Where Emerson, Manitoba, is today, on the Red River. The officers in the Great March West assembled here before trekking west, making their final preparations and outfitting themselves for the arduous journey that lay ahead.

Fort Ellice: Northwest of Fort Dufferin, this first NWMP headquarters had long been a Hudson's Bay Company post. It was named after Edward Ellice, an HBC official.

Fort Macleod: West of Fort Whoop-up and south of present-day Calgary, this second NWMP headquarters was constructed by and named after the second commissioner, James Macleod, in 1876. The Métis guide Jerry Potts led Macleod to this cottonwood-forested spot at the junction of the St. Mary's and Oldman rivers.

Fort Pelly: On the Swan River, briefly the location of NWMP headquarters. The site was a snake-infested marshy area.

Fort Pitt: Site of an old HBC post and later an NWMP sub-post, near Onion Lake, Saskatchewan.

Fort Walsh: Fort Walsh, Saskatchewan, named after Superintendent James Morrow Walsh. It was the NWMP post established in the Cypress Hills in 1875 and abandoned in 1882.

Fort Whoop-up: The most notorious of several whiskey-trading posts in the new western territory. It was illegal to sell liquor to the Natives in American territory, so the traders came north to ply their trade in the lawless territory area north of Montana.

Frog Lake: Site of a massacre in April 1885 that was part of the Northwest Rebellion. The small settlement at Frog Lake was attacked by Cree war chief Wandering Spirit and his warriors.

Mistowasis: Name of a Cree Indian chief.

Milky River: The Milk River, which flows from northern Montana into what is now Alberta.

Oldman River: The Oldman River in southwestern Alberta was the site of Fort Macleod.
Pelly River: This river in the Yukon Territory was explored and mapped by Inspector J.D. Moodie in 1897.
Roche Percée: The first overland leg of the Great March West was from Fort Dufferin on the Red River to Roche Percée, near the border of the Dakota Territory. By the time the officers reached Roche Percée, about a third of their planned journey, Commissioner French split up the group, sending the sickest ones to the nearest supply centre, Fort Ellice, and from there to Fort Edmonton. This group was led by Inspector W.D. Jarvis.
Rockcliffe: A suburb of Ottawa, the site of the RCMP Musical Ride (Canadian Sunset Ceremony).
St. Anne: South of modern-day Winnipeg.
Sweet Grass Hills: South of Fort Whoop-up, in the northern Montana Territory. A resting place on the Great March West.
St. Vito: San Vito, a town in Sicily in the area where the No. 1 Provost Company, a 79-man unit of the First Canadian infantry division, was posted in the Second World War.
Touchwood Hills: Located in present-day south-central Saskatchewan; the HBC Touchwood Hills fur-trading post was built here in 1879.
Whiskey Gap: A whiskey trading post south of Fort Macleod near the present-day U.S. border.
Wild Horse: Today, a border-crossing point between Alberta and Montana.
Writing: Possibly a reference to Riding Mountain in western Manitoba, now the location of a museum dedicated to the NWMP.

RCMP or Military Terms

Blacksnake: A heavy whip made of braided leather.
Fistic: Having to do with fist fighting.
H.L.: Hard labour.
T.T.: Teetotal.
Mud fatigue: Dirty work.
Guidon: A flag used for signalling carried by soldiers in a parade, or the soldier who carries it.
O.C.: Officer Commanding, another term for Commanding Officer.
Sick Parade: The reporting of persons needing medical attention.
Seventy-Nine: Member of the 79-man unit of the Provost police posted in Italy in the Second World War. One of its duties was to keep the traffic flowing safely on the treacherous roads.
Picquet: Guard duty.

Obscure Terms

Amalgamator: A machine used in separating metal from ore.
Cayuse: An Indian pony (or a native American of Oregon).
Piute: A native of the southwestern U.S.
Shaganappi thong: Strap, thong, or cord made from rawhide.
Coyote: Another word for a wild horse.
Grub-pile or grub-stake: Food stash.
Jumper sleigh: Horse sleigh.
Jumpers: Horses.

Old blind pig: Speakeasy.

Sourdough: A prospector or pioneer of northwestern Canada, or an inhabitant of Alaska or the Yukon.

Spalpeen: An Irish term for a scamp, or ne'er-do-well.

Stamp mill: A machine or mill for pulverizing ore.

Tick: Credit.

Toe-head scrub: Shrubbery.

Vag: A vagrancy charge.

Vide: Latin term for "See."

Wedding-yoke: Newly married.

Yegg: A burglar, especially one who robs safes.

Characters

Atty Irvine: The third commissioner of the force, Colonel Acheson Gosford Irvine was part of the Red River expedition in 1870.

Crozier: Assistant Commissioner Lief Newry Crozier became the tenth officer in the NWMP in November 1873. He marched west in 1874 and was posted to Fort Macleod. In 1879 he took over as superintendent from Major Walsh in the Cypress Hills.

French Chartrand: Constable Albert Joseph "Frenchie" Chartrand, a crew member of the *St. Roch* on its historic voyage through the North West Passage.

Jerry Potts: Potts, a Métis guide, met Major James Macleod at Fort Benton, Montana, in 1874 and served as his scout and interpreter, leading him to the site of the Oldman River, where Fort Macleod was built.

Jim Macleod: Second commissioner James Macleod, appointed in 1876 after Commissioner French resigned, established peaceful relations with the First Nations.

W.R. May (aka Wop): a bush pilot who helped track down the Mad Trapper of Rat River.

Millen: Constable Edgar Millen was shot dead by the Mad Trapper of Rat River in 1932.

Steele: Major-General Sir Samuel Benfield Steele, probably the best-known member of the NWMP, was on the Great March. He was with the group diverted from Roche Percée to Fort Edmonton under Inspector Jarvis.

Walsh: On the Great March West in 1874, Superintendent James Walsh commanded the "D" division. In 1875 he and his men built a fort in the Cypress Hills that was named after him.

Wood: Assistant Commissioner Zachary Taylor Wood, great-grandson of the twelfth U.S. president, Zachary Taylor, served in the Northwest Rebellion.

RCMP Ranks

Special Constable (S/Cst.)
Constable (Cst.)
Corporal (Cpl.)
Sergeant (Sgt.)
Inspector (Insp.)
Superintendent (Supt.)
Assistant Commissioner (A/Commr.)
Commissioner (Commr.)

SOURCES

RCMP Veterans' Association *Scarlet and Gold.* Vancouver, BC: 1919
    through 1996.
The RCMP Quarterly. Ottawa, ON: 1933 through 2001.
Wake the Prairie Echoes. Saskatchewan History and Folklore Society,
    Western Producer Book Service. Saskatoon, SK: 1973.

PHOTO CREDITS

p. 9: Heritage House Collection
p. 45: Glenbow-Alberta Institute
p. 61: Heritage House Collection
p. 85: Heritage House Collection
p. 111: Cecil Clark
p. 137: Glenbow Library, NA-1480-31
p. 163: Royal Canadian Mounted Police

Edgar Arthur Kuhn was born November 7, 1932, on a farm near Bromhead, Saskatchewan. His family moved to a farm south of Midale, Saskatchewan, where he grew up and graduated from high school. He joined the RCMP in August 1952 and was given regimental number 17871. He subsequently served six years in British Columbia, six years in the Northwest Territories, and over thirteen years in Saskatchewan. He retired in 1978 with over 25 years of service and was awarded the RCMP Long Service medal. He also worked for thirteen years  for Saskatchewan Government Insurance as an auto adjuster and licence issuer.

Kuhn has written articles on criminal cases for *RCMP Quarterly* magazine, a book on the life and times of his father, and *Ellesmere Land: A Mountie in the High Arctic*.

Although he is not a poet, his interest in collecting police poetry dates back more than 30 years. Edgar and his wife, Claire, have raised five children, have numerous grandchildren, and live in Weyburn, Saskatchewan.